Is it all in your mind?

A 10 step plan that really works for anxiety and depression

Is it all in your mind?

A 10 step plan that really works for anxiety and depression

Charmaine Shepherd

ISBN 978-1-4477-5678-1

Acknowledgements

This book is dedicated to my soul mate and partner who never gave up on me when I was as low as could be; who taught me how to recognise resilience, determination and courage in myself. This book is a combination of my own experience in tackling depression and anxiety, as well as the wonderful teachings from a few very remarkable healers. Firstly, professor Ang who taught me all I need to know about acupuncture; and all the other teachers that I have had along the way. To the amazing team that I work with now Mo, Janet and Jenny, thank you for making the holistic approach to treatment a reality! Lastly, I would like to express my gratitude to Bianca Marais for her tireless encouragement and editing.

All names in this book have been changed and certain situations changed for patient protection.

Contents

Acknowledgements v

Preface ix

Introduction...xi

Chapter 1. Do you suffer from depression, anxiety or panic attacks? 1

Chapter 2. Brain matters – is it all in my mind?...........................5

Chapter 3. What may be causing my depression or anxiety?........23

Chapter 4. Medications are not always the answer 59

Chapter 5. What's the fix?...63

Chapter 6. Helpful Therapies 87

Chapter 7. Traditional Chinese Medicine and Acupuncture 101

Chapter 8. Emotional well-being...121

Chapter 9. Lifestyle contributors...141

10 Step Plan 145

In conclusion..147

Recommended Reading List 149

Index..151

Preface

I have battled with depression since the age of 14, or maybe even long before that. At first I did not realise that I was depressed. I would quite often not feel able to get out of bed to go to school or see my friends, yet it was something I had to fight. In time I learned to wear a mask that would hide how I really felt from the world, but inside I felt dead, desperate and terribly misunderstood.

I hid from the world through a series of illnesses. I had glandular fever that kept me away from school for several weeks, and after that I would bounce from one illness to the next, until eventually my doctor referred me to a psychologist who labelled me a hypochondriac. The illnesses I got were the only way to shield me from the world. They were my escape. Soon after that, the anxiety started. I started worrying about whether I was really a hypochondriac; did I have a mental condition? By the time I was 18, I was diagnosed with depression and began my long journey with anti-depressants and anti-anxiety medications. At first the anti-depressants worked, but after a while their effectiveness would wane. In some cases I had very unpleasant side-effects from the medications. Also, I wanted to find answers. Why was I depressed? Was there something wrong with my mind, or did I somehow bring this on myself? Was there anyone else to blame?

I plodded through university on my chemical cocktails of Prozac (or whatever the prescription at the time would have been) and somehow managed to get myself a good job at a national Science Council. However, I knew that at some point I would have to address this looming problem which kept creeping up at me. I also felt that I could no longer keep up the mask that I had worn for family, colleagues and friends for all those years. At one of the lowest points in my life, I decided that I was going to take a job overseas to escape from the pressure and expectations of family and friends and a broken relationship. So I took up a position in Switzerland working for a pharmaceutical software company.

It was here that I met my husband. When I worked up the courage to explain how I had been plagued by depression and anxiety, he vowed to help me fight it. He gave me the courage to take responsibility for myself, and to get to the bottom of why this was happening to me, rather than to hide behind anti-depressants. That's when I began to seriously research depression. In the years that followed, I made changes to my lifestyle that would gradually lift the depression, and with each small step I gained confidence that I could do this for myself. I still think that it has been the best thing I could ever have done; a personal gift from me to me. I've learned an enormous amount about who I am, and I've also learned to like myself a great deal more. I discovered too that I have much more resilience than I thought I ever had. I now know what will bring on or trigger my depression, and what I need to do to keep my mental health in good condition. But most importantly, I've learned that it's all up to me!

Since then, I have been lucky enough to have two very special individuals in my life. Professor T.T. Ang in Singapore who guided me through my acupuncture studies for 3 years, and who gave so much of his time to explaining the physiology of emotions to me. I have also been blessed to work alongside a team of dedicated therapists whose focus and insight into the minds and souls of people has always been an inspiration. These extraordinary individuals have shaped the way in which I work with patients today.

Now when I see patients, I often remember where I was when I began this journey, and I know that there is hope. In working with people, I always hope to gently guide them, while still letting them find the way for themselves. For it is when we learn to achieve full control over our lives that we can learn to live in this world and fully engage with life.

Introduction

Anxiety and depression can make us feel like strangers to ourselves and the world. These conditions separate us from ourselves and affect our work, relationships, creativity and passion for life! Many of us will learn to wear a mask to the outside world to hide these paralyzing conditions from others, but we'll live with the knowledge within ourselves that something is askew. Others will withdraw into themselves leaving family, and themselves, alienated. However you may have responded to anxiety and depression, your reaction would have profoundly affected the way in which you engage with life and those around you. If you feel this way, you may be comforted to know that you are not alone. New statistics show that these conditions are endemic, and more and more people in the United Kingdom are now asking for help.

Mental health conditions have abysmal effects not only for the individual and their immediate family, but also for society as a whole. Figures from the Statistics office of the UK government show that one in six people will at some point in their life succumb to anxiety and depression. A report from the Sainsbury Centre for Mental Health has put the total cost of mental health problems in England alone at more than £77 billion a year. This figure takes into account the healthcare burden on the NHS as well as private care. It also incorporates the economic effect of stress, depression or anxiety. More specifically, depression accounts for the loss of more than 100 million working days in the UK each year and tragically more than 2,615 deaths per year are due to depression.

This book has been written to look at some of the underlying causes of depression and anxiety, the most common mental health issues faced by most people these days. We will explore some of the less known causes of mental illness, in particular the gut connection with the mind.

In this book, many effective therapies for combating depression and anxiety are presented. We'll look at real cases where hopeless despair has been transformed into possibility, and where anxiety has transformed into peace! My hope is that the book will offer readers the opportunity to explore possible causes for their depression and anxiety and empower them to make changes that will offer long-lasting relief.

People always ask me what determines a successful treatment outcome. The answer is simple: those people who take control of their condition, and who are empowered to do so, will always find strategies to overcome depression and anxiety. If you can make the choice to take back control and take charge of your own course, rather than rely on medications or professionals to just 'sort things' for you, you will no doubt be on the road to recovery. It may not be an easy journey, but if you follow the pointers you will no doubt get there! There is always, of course, a need for expert help and advice, but at all times we must question the obvious and take charge of our own course.

Since childhood I have struggled with both anxiety and depression and have fought to try and understand these conditions. When I was younger I was continuously prescribed anti-depressants and anti-anxiety medications. At the time, I felt resigned to a life of depression which the medications barely concealed from myself and others. Lucky for me, I did not respond very well to these medications and so I had no choice but to find solutions for myself! This book is a compilation of what I've learned through my own experience, through my study of acupuncture, working with world leaders such as Professor Ang and also what I see working for my patients every day.

CHAPTER 1

Do you suffer from depression, anxiety or panic attacks?

If you are reading this book, you are probably affected by anxiety, depression or panic attacks. Although there are resources available to you to find out whether you are "officially" depressed or anxious, I am less interested in the labels that people are given. Rather than worry about what you have been labelled, I suggest that if you experience anything that is described below, you would probably benefit from reading further.

Depression and low moods

People suffering from depression often feel worthless, guilty, sad or disinterested in life. Commonly, people will find a change in sleeping habits. This can often come about as a result of a change in life circumstance or loss. People describe feeling detached from life, suffering low moods and feeling that they don't have the zest to pursue the things that they want.

The many spectrums of depression vary from severe clinical depression to milder forms of periodic or constant low moods. It is important to know that most people will at times experience low moods, especially when life throws its curve balls at you, but if your low moods continue for more than a few weeks and begin to affect your work or relationships; it is advisable to find help.

Sometimes low moods, and not necessarily depression, can prevent people from reaching for their dreams. Often people are not aware that their moods are low, but friends or family around them notice that they slowly give up on their dreams. James (a media consultant) came in for acupuncture on a problem knee. As we were talking I sensed that James's mood was low. He told me that he dreams of a major career change that involves humanitarian work but there were always obstacles. Now he even doubted whether his idea was viable at all. He had the family support and encouragement to back him, but somehow he had lost his grasp on this dream. I offered a sounding board and his idea sounded very workable. He denied that he was depressed, but he had over a time given up on all his dreams.

He had just lost confidence, and as a result was stuck in a job that he did not enjoy. We decided to do a Resonance Biofeedback session to look for underlying reasons for his mood. I then prescribed some herbal medicines and dietary changes and James got his "fire" back. A few weeks later he had quit his job and was running around frantically getting his dream going. I still occasionally see James, and we talk about how he managed to make the change over into doing something he is so passionate about. Looking back he can see that there was an element of depression of which he was not aware. In James' case, it took just a simple remedy and a dietary change to get him "back into the game". It always reminds me how connected the mind and body are, and that often it requires just a little tweak to set something big into motion.

Depression Checklist:

1. Difficulty sleeping or finding you need more sleep than usual
2. Lack of concentration
3. Not having the energy to do the things you used to
4. Change in appetite and weight
5. Lacking motivation for things you usually enjoy
6. Feeling agitated or anxious
7. Thoughts of suicide
8. Feelings of worthlessness or guilt

If you experience more than four of the above, you could possibly have an element of depression.

Anxiety

All of us will experience anxiety in our lives. For example, nervousness about an exam or a driving test is a normal reaction to the stresses of life. However, if you find that there is a feeling of unease, fear or impending doom which is not proportionate to the situation you face, you may be suffering from anxiety. If anxiety is interfering with your life, and you have changed lifestyle to accommodate your anxiety, you do need to reach out for help.

Anxiety can stop people from achieving their goals. Jane, a student, came to see me regarding anxiety. She had stopped going to a certain lecture because her stomach tied in knots each time she entered the class. Suddenly dread would overcome her. There was no rational reason to feel this way; she had a good academic track record and was not struggling with the subject material. Each time Jane went into the lecture her hands became clammy, her heart raced, her stomach felt knotty and she found it very difficult to concentrate. Eventually she no longer could attend this class. This was clearly not going to help her get through her studies, so we had to act quickly and find a solution that would get her back into class. A few weeks later, with the anxiety pattern broken using acupuncture, she comfortably sat through lectures and went on to achieve a distinction! If you have similar feelings to Jane about any situation which is keeping you from doing the things you would like to do, you may be experiencing anxiety.

I also believe that when our energy is directed into fear and anxiety, we are not free to live and love life. It takes so much energy from the body to keep the anxiety wheel going, that there is very little left to enjoy life.

Panic attacks!

Panic attacks are repeated, unexpected episodes during which you suddenly are overcome by intense fear or discomfort. These episodes can create some very uncomfortable symptoms that include:

- A pounding heartbeat
- trembling

- shaking
- sweating
- shortness of breath or difficulty breathing
- chest pain
- a feeling of nausea
- abdominal discomfort or pain
- jelly legs
- a feeling of numbness
- feelings of unreality or detachment

Panic attacks are not a sign that you are going crazy. It is true that you may feel out of control, but the symptoms are in fact very different from those of any mental illness. These episodes are exactly the same as those of a person in extreme physical danger. The body has merely sent a distress signal which has sent you into fight and flight. The fear is then maintained by your feelings and emotions in response to the panic.

Later on, we will list some ways in which you can respond which will minimize the fear during a panic attack.

With coping mechanisms in place, it is possible to learn to minimise the effect of panic on the body. Liz was brought in by a close friend who was concerned about her. She was suffering from chronic and debilitating panic attacks, and as a result she had made several changes in her life. She recently started cancelling social events and an annual girls' holiday with friends. Liz felt that she was going crazy as her body was going into fight and flight at just the thought of going on holiday. We were never able to ascertain why the panic attacks began in the first place, but we began to work on developing new patterns for her nervous system. A few months on I was glad to receive a postcard from Liz posted from Spain saying only "No panic attacks. Thank you!"

Although anxiety itself may hold individuals back from beginning treatment, doing so can bring enormous relief and can be life-changing. Many individuals with anxiety are afraid of starting any form of treatment as they anticipate a worsening of their condition. However, overcoming panic can be very liberating.

CHAPTER 2

Brain matters – is it all in my mind?

The brain is an intricate network of electrical signals and chemical reactions. For optimal mental functioning, the 'electrical' circuits or 'wiring' must work smoothly. At the same time the 'chemical mixture' must be just right. There are several things that contribute to the mental changes that occur during depression and anxiety. When depression or anxiety strikes, it is accompanied by changes in the electrochemical functioning of the brain. Firstly, even tiny biochemical shifts within the brain neurotransmitters or receptors can alter the chemical "mix". In turn this affects the electrical signalling, altering the 'wiring' of the nervous system. This Chapter looks at how the brain functions.

The Brain

The brain is made up of about a hundred billion neural cells. Each of these cells is wired to other cells within the brain and body by nerve fibres. About 4 million miles of nerve fibres exist in the brain, constantly transmitting messages between cells. While I am typing the words on this page, cells in my brains are generating the thoughts, putting them into words, and sending signals through the nerve pathways to my fingers so that the muscles move in such a way that I type the right keys at the right time. My eyes, reading what is coming up on the screen are sending feedback to the brain and so I go back and correct the bits where my fingers got it wrong. The nerve fibres that connect cells continuously send messages or signals day and night, regulating millions of actions in the body at one time. In the same way, cells within the brain communicate constantly, with cells throughout the body. It is well known that depression affects the way in which the physical body functions. At the same time, physical illness can contribute to depression. This is a very important point to remember when looking at depression, we must look not only at the mind's role in its development and treatment, but take on a more holistic approach.

Nerve cells communicate by moving chemical messengers across a small gap called a synapse. These chemical messengers are called **neurotransmitters**. The neurotransmitters are picked up by receptors on the receiving nerve cell, triggering an electric signal (Image 1).

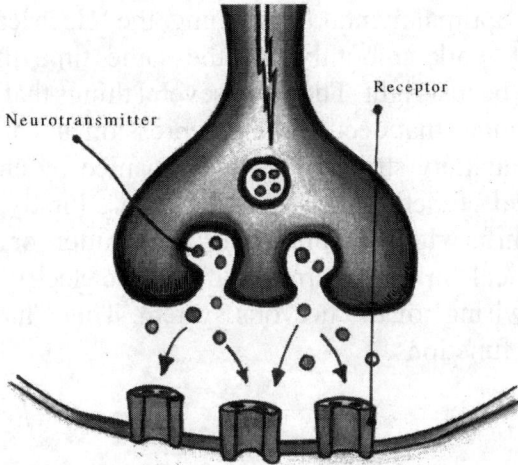

Image 1: Neurotransmitters travel to receptors to trigger a signal

Neurochemical functioning

Subtle chemical changes or shifts in the neurotransmitters, or their receptors, can alter the electrochemical pattern of the brain and influence the way in which we think, feel and behave. In other words, change the mixture of neurotransmitters and we change our brain chemistry. This is an amazing, yet frightening thought. We know for instance, that certain chemicals interfere with neurotransmitters or their receptors leading to curious effects. It is well known that some anti-depressants, such as Paroxetine, which concentrate the amount of serotonin in the synapses can trigger suicidal or violent behaviour. Other drugs can induce either euphoria or depression in different people; amphetamine being a good example. In other words, any substance that changes brain chemistry can change the way we think and feel!

Neurotransmitters

Most people have heard of the well-studied neurotransmitters such as serotonin and dopamine as they are given a lot of attention in the media. These chemical messengers have been linked to mood and behaviour and they are the golden nuggets that the pharmaceutical industry is after! In this section we will look at the functions of just a few of these neurotransmitters: dopamine, serotonin, noradrenalin, acetylcholine and gamma-aminobutyric acid (GABA). In the right balance, the neurotransmitters ensure a healthy and happy mind. An imbalance, however, leads to emotional disorders, anxiety and/or depression. For example, deficiencies in serotonin availability have been linked to depression, anxiety, irregular appetite, aggression and even pain.

Let's look at the functions of some of the more common neurotransmitters:

GABA

Gamma-aminobutyric acid (luckily shortened to GABA) acts like a brake on the brain, slowing down activity of the nerve cells throughout the body. People who regularly meditate are known to have increased levels of the neurotransmitter GABA and as a result, their brains (and bodies) are less excitable. This neurotransmitter is best known for stabilizing mood disorders and

GABA
▪ Acts as a "brake" on the brain
▪ Slows down brain activity, stabilizes the mood and induces relaxation
▪ Lowered levels results in anxiety, racing thoughts, insomnia and addictions
▪ Beef, pork, sesame and sunflower seeds contain glutamine which is necessary for its synthesis

inducing relaxation. By reducing excitability of the nerves, it has a calming effect on the entire system. When there is insufficient GABA, it is thought that anxiety, tension and insomnia results. Individuals with low GABA levels find it difficult to fall asleep at night because of "mind chatter". Having lowered levels of this neurotransmitter in the brain is like driving a car without brakes. In the same way, people with lowered GABA levels feel that their minds are racing out of control and they cannot find the "brake".

Addictions also commonly arise when GABA levels are lowered as the addictive substance provides an escape from an overactive mind. Alcohol, for instance, has the effect of binding directly to the GABA receptors, thus activating the relaxation or sedating effect. So, for those individuals with lowered GABA, the craving for alcohol is understandable as it offers them relief from unabated tension. Unfortunately, alcohol is not a healthy solution. Apart from the undesirable social effects of alcohol, in time the GABA receptors become resistant to alcohol, thus requiring larger amounts of the substance to create the same effect. Alcohol use then becomes chronic, which has widespread negative effects on the body.

We do not know why GABA levels are lowered in some individuals, but it is thought that there may be a genetic element involved, implying that we "inherit" the tendency for low GABA from our parents. Trauma is also thought to lower GABA levels. In addition, poor nutrition may result in the body lacking the "building blocks" for making GABA. To synthesize GABA, the body uses an amino acid called Glutamine which can be found in beef, pork, sesame seeds and sunflower seeds.

Serotonin

Most people have heard of serotonin. It is the feel-good neurotransmitter that influences mood and behavior in many ways. Serotonin enables relaxation by returning the nervous system and mind to its homeostatic 'set point'. In other words, serotonin has balancing and regulating properties on widespread functions throughout the body including mood, appetite, sleep, muscle contraction, memory and learning. Most people are surprised to learn that this neurotransmitter is responsible for regulating intestinal movements and that nearly 90% of all the body's serotonin can be

Serotonin
<ul><li>Serotonin is the "feel good" neurotransmitter</li><li>Regulates intestinal movements</li><li>Gut problems can affect serotonin production just as low serotonin affects the gut</li><li>Regulates mood, appetite, sleep, muscle contraction, memory and learning</li><li>Low levels linked to depression, obesity, insomnia, sleep disturbance, headaches, migraine, premenstrual tension and Fibromyalgia</li><li>Synthesis requires tryptophan, iron and vitamin B3</li></ul>

found in the gut! It is no wonder then that the gut and the mind are so closely connected; the link between serotonin levels and gut health is well researched and there is a close connection between the health of the gut and that of the mind. Later on in the section "What may be causing my depression or anxiety" the concept will be fully explored. For now it is enough to know that a gut imbalance is often an underlying cause of depression.

Low serotonin levels are also linked to depression, obesity, insomnia, narcolepsy, sleep apnea, migraine headaches, premenstrual syndrome and Fibromyalgia. Most modern anti-depressants work by increasing the amount of serotonin available in the synapses, not the production of serotonin itself. Serotonin production within the body relies on the amino acid tryptophan as well as other co-factors (or nutrients) needed to make the conversion.

A deficiency in either the amino acid tryptophan or the co-factors (iron, vitamin B3, magnesium etc) will result in lowered levels of serotonin (and melatonin). Sources of tryptophan include chocolate, oats, mangoes, dried dates, yogurt, cottage cheese, red meat, eggs, fish, poultry, sesame, chickpeas, sunflower seeds, pumpkin seeds and spirulina.

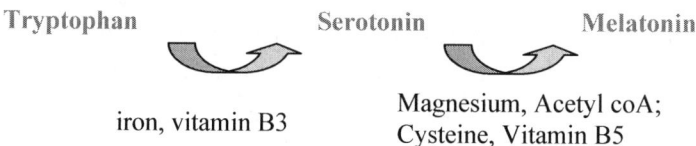

Tryptophan   Serotonin   Melatonin

iron, vitamin B3

Magnesium, Acetyl coA;
Cysteine, Vitamin B5

Serotonin and Melatonin Synthesis

Dopamine

Dopamine plays an important part in behavior and cognition, motor activity, motivation and reward, sleep, mood, attention and learning. This is the neurotransmitter that we usually associate with Parkinson's Disease (PD). Individuals affected by PD experience symptoms as a result of loss of the nerve cells in the region of the brain that produce Dopamine. As a result they become Dopamine depleted which results in the muscle rigidity and loss of controlled movements seen in PD patients. Because of Dopamine's effect on mood, most people affected by Parkinson's struggle with chronic depression.

Dopamine
<ul><li>Involved in mood, cognition, motor activity, motivation, reward, sleep, attention and learning</li><li>Provides motivation to perform activities rewarded by pleasure e.g. sex</li><li>Also linked to addictions especially cocaine and amphetamines</li><li>Synthesis requires phenylalanine, Iron and vitamin B3</li><li>Sources of phenylalanine: chicken, turkey, fish, almonds, avocado, banana, pumpkin and sesame seeds</li></ul>

Dopamine is also involved in the experience of pleasure and provides motivation for individuals to perform certain activities. Dopamine is released by naturally rewarding experiences such as food, sex and drugs, reinforcing the pleasurable experience. It is not surprising then that Dopamine is also linked to addiction.

Dopamine is also the driver that excites people, drives motivation and goal setting. On the physical plane it is associated with blood pressure, metabolism and digestion.

Tyrosine, which can be synthesized in the body from the amino acid Phenylalanine is the precursor to Dopamine and requires both iron and vitamin B3 for its conversion. Phenylalanine is found mainly in high protein foods such as chicken, oats, walnuts, cottage cheese, turkey, fish, almonds, avocado, banana, yoghurts, pumpkin and sesame seeds.

Phenylanaline

Tyrosine   **Dopamine**

iron, Vitamin B3

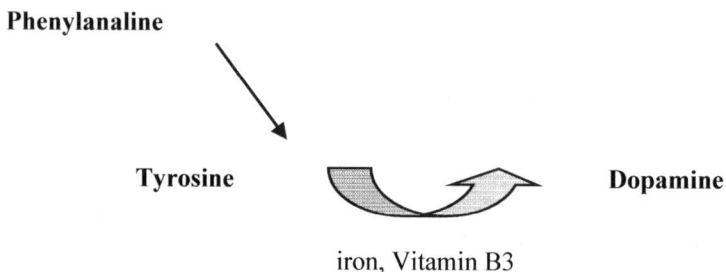

Dopamine synthesis

Street drugs such as cocaine and amphetamine both markedly affect this neurotransmitter. In fact, investigators at St. Jude Children's Research Hospital have found a relationship between cocaine use and the development of PD later in life. In their findings, they also found that pregnant women who use cocaine increase the risk of their children to develop PD.

It is also interesting to note that patients with PD often suffer from severe depression and very sluggish bowels, a brain-gut connection which will be explained in detail later.

Noradrenaline

Noradrenaline is commonly known for its role in the physical manifestations of fight and flight such as increasing the heart rate and blood pressure. Several research studies, however, have also linked the levels of the neurotransmitter noradrenalin to motivation and drive. A recent study published

Noradrenaline
<ul><li>Linked to motivation, drive, positive self perception</li><li>Gives us the ability to push forward to achieve our goals and dreams</li><li>Low levels linked to lack of direction, or having dreams/goals, none of which come to fruition.</li><li>Synthesised from Dopamine; requires Tyrosine, iron, vitamin B3, vitamin C and copper</li></ul>

in the journal of the European College of Neuropsychopharmacology clearly indicated the difference between the function of serotonin and noradrenalin. Researchers gave patients with severe depression either only a standard anti-depressant that increases serotonin availability (Selective Serotonin Reuptake Inhibitor or SSRI) or in combination with a drug that increases concentrations of Noradrenaline (Noradrenaline Reuptake inhibitor or NARI). The study showed that the patients taking the SSRI had an increase in mood, but those taking the NARI also faired better in terms of motivation and drive. Those taking the NARI also showed an improvement in negative self perception. What this means is that noradrenaline levels may be key to our levels of self esteem and our motivation to push forward on dreams and goals. It may be the "mojo" of neurotransmitters. As noradrenalin provides us with the 'drive', low levels of noradrenalin are associated with people who have ideas, none of which come to fruition. In the body, Noradrenaline is created from Dopamine through a conversion which requires vitamin C and copper.

phenylalanine   tyrosine   **Dopamine**   **Noradrenaline**

iron, vitamin B3   Copper and Vitamin C

Noradrenaline and Dopamine conversion

A copper and vitamin C deficiency is rare and conversion problems may be more likely due to insufficient iron or vitamin B3 (also called Niacin) levels. Iron is found abundantly in red meat, fish, poultry, beans, leafy vegetables, lentils, tofu, chickpeas and black-eyed peas. More commonly occurring in women, iron deficiency can leave the person utterly fatigued and depressed. Good sources of vitamin B3 (Niacin) include liver, beef, pork and prawns. Although higher concentrations exist in meat products, it is possible to get Niacin from seeds and almonds, rice bran, beans, green vegetables, turnips, carrots, and celery. Oh, I can just picture some of you heading for the kitchen for a liver fry up, mumbling something about mojo! But on a serious note, nutritional deficiencies can profoundly affect our mental functioning and make a difference between lacking luster and having that sparkle.

Acetylcholine

Acetylcholine has very wide-ranging effects on the central nervous system such as memory, arousal and excitability. This neurotransmitter can be found in the brain, neuromuscular junctions, spinal cord and throughout the nervous system. In the brain, acetylcholine improves memory and alertness.

Low levels of acetylcholine have been associated with an inability to connect memories. For instance, you may know a person's face but cannot remember the name. Much of today's research in Alzheimer's disease, as well as age-related memory decline, focuses on the role of acetylcholine in storing, retrieving and connecting memories. Individuals with low acetylcholine usually have poor dream recall, difficulty concentrating, a dry mouth and exhaustion.

To make Acetylcholine, the body requires a nutrient called choline. The body is capable of making only small amounts of choline, so dietary intake is still necessary. Choline is found abundantly in egg yolks, soy, wheat germ and liver.

Acetylcholine
▪ Linked to excitability, arousal and memory, alertness
▪ Found in the brain, neuromuscular junctions, spinal cord
▪ Low levels linked to inability to connect memories, poor dream recall, difficulty concentrating, exhaustion
▪ Associated with Alzheimer's disease
▪ Choline is the building block of acetylcholine and is found in eggs, soy, wheat germ, and liver

Melatonin

Melatonin is a hormone manufactured in the brain by the pineal gland, from the amino acid tryptophan. Just before bedtime, increased melatonin is released into the blood stream and is linked with peaceful sleep. Stress, however, is known to reduce melatonin and disturbed sleep patterns can be an indicator of both depression and anxiety.

Melatonin
▪ Major regulator of sleep
▪ Antioxidant
▪ Prevents and slows down cancer growth
▪ Linked to SAD and bipolar disorder
▪ Produced in darkness, inhibited by the light
▪ Melatonin is synthesized from the amino acid tryptophan
▪ Food sources of tryptophan: chocolate, oats, bananas, dried dates, cottage cheese, meat, fish and turkey

Melatonin is also called the hormone of darkness as it is released in the dark, and inhibited by light. Up until recent history, man was not exposed to as much artificial light as we are now and this increased artificial light alters melatonin levels. If you're not sleeping well and are anxious, chances are that your melatonin levels are lowered.

Melatonin is linked to the prevention of cancer and slowing down its rate of growth. Researchers at the State University of Ohio have shown that women who have light filtering through into their bedrooms at night have a higher risk of developing breast cancer. In a study involving 643 cancer patients using melatonin supplementation, a significantly reduced incidence of cancer-related death was recorded. Although we don't know the exact mechanism, it would appear that its anti-cancer properties cannot be only explained by its role as an antioxidant.

Light suppresses the release of melatonin and even low levels of street lighting could interfere with Melatonin production, causing a deficiency of this critical neurotransmitter. For those individuals with sleep disturbances, blackout blinds/curtains are essential. Even turning lights on for a few minutes during the middle of the night can cause Melatonin levels to drop drastically, so resist the temptation to read if you cannot fall asleep!

Melatonin imbalances have been linked to Seasonal Affective Disorder (SAD) and supplementation with this hormone, when there is deficiency, can be very effective. At the time of writing this, Melatonin is only available on prescription in the United Kingdom, although it can be purchased over the counter in many other countries. Mental disorders in which the circadian rhythms are affected, such as bipolar disorder, also responds to Melatonin treatment.

Melatonin (and serotonin) can be boosted through diet. Foods such as chocolate (make sure its at least 70% dark chocolate), oats, bananas, sesame seeds, chickpeas, sunflower seeds, dried dates, cottage cheese, meat, fish, turkey and peanuts contain a component called tryptophan which the body uses to make serotonin and melatonin. Later on, we'll look more at how the diet affects our neurotransmitters but it is important to keep in mind that we have to give the body the right building blocks to be able to form the neurotransmitters.

Getting the balance right

Table 1 shows how important the right balance of the neurotransmitters is. If the brain has too little serotonin you will feel depressed, too much and you may feel headaches or nausea. Too little noradrenalin and you feel depressed and unmotivated, too much and you are jittery and anxious. It's a fine balance to get right! Luckily, the body has many mechanisms in place which regulate the production, use and breakdown of these neurotransmitters. The problem arises, however, when certain chemicals in our food or environment sends the balance askew.

Neurotransmitter	Action	Excess Neurotransmitter	Deficiency of Neurotransmitter
Serotonin	Mood, emotions, temperature regulation, sleep/wake cycles	Headaches, migraine, nausea	Depression, clouded thinking
Dopamine	Muscle tension, perceptions, sorting out what is real/important/imaginary, reward, sleep mood, ability to experience pleasure and pain	Overactive brain, seeing or imagining things e.g. schizophrenia Cocaine causes increased levels of dopamine	Muscular tightness, depression, cravings, sleep disturbance,

Neurotransmitter	Action	Excess Neurotransmitter	Deficiency of Neurotransmitter
Noradrenalin	Motivation, drive, sleep patterns, mood, emotions, self perception, affects blood pressure	Anxious, jittery, high blood pressure	Depressed, low blood pressure, poor self perception, lacking "drive"
Acetylcholine	Used in the body to make muscles contract, in the brain it controls arousal, memory and learning	Muscle tightness	Confusion, slow at learning, poor memory, poor dream recall, dry mouth
GABA	Acts like a brake, slowing the brain down, stabilizes mood, induces relaxation	Sedated or drowsy	Anxious, excited and racing thoughts, panic disorder, insomnia, tension
Melatonin	Circadian rhythms, induces sleep, dreaming, antioxidant, hormonal regulation	headaches, nausea, irritability, nightmares, hormone imbalance	Obesity, insomnia, headaches, memory, sleep disorder, SAD, sexual dysfunction

Table 1: Neurotransmitter functions, excesses and deficiencies

Although the neurotransmitters have been discussed individually in the section above, they often have overlapping roles and a complex interplay of actions. As a result, they have many overlapping functions and their interactions are often blurred.

Noradrenalin   **Serotonin**

Anxiety
Irritability
Impulsiveness

Vigilance
Alertness
Concentration

Obsessions
Compulsions
Sleep

Cognition
Emotions
Moods

Libido
Appetite
Aggression

motivation

Pleasure
Motivation
Drive

Dopamine

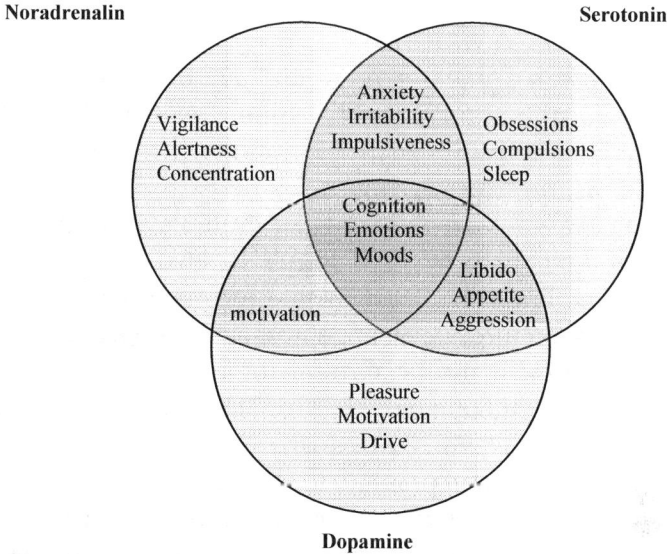

Overlapping roles of neurotransmitters

For optimal functioning, the mind requires the right proportions of neurotransmitters and science is not yet close to understanding the complexity of their interactions. The body has very intelligent and complex mechanisms for regulating the production of neurotransmitters, given the right building blocks. When we interfere with the mixture in the form of medications, drugs and environmental chemicals, the balance gets upset, leading to a variety of mental and physical symptoms (or side-effects in the case of medication).

The regions of the brain

"From the brain and the brain alone arise our pleasures, joys, laughter and jests, as well as our sorrows, pains and griefs"

Hippocrates

The brain is a very complex structure, but for our purposes we'll only look at the Limbic system which is linked to anxiety and depression.

Limbic system

Those who research clinical depression have been interested in a particular part of the brain called the limbic system. This area of the brain regulates activities such as emotions, physical and sexual drives as well as the stress response.

There are various structures of the limbic system that are of particular importance. The **hypothalamus** is a small structure located at the base of the brain. It is responsible for many basic functions such as body temperature, sleep, appetite, sexual drive and the stress reaction. It is also the control centre for some of the key hormones. The hypothalamus, although only the size of an almond, controls the nervous system and metabolism, and when disrupted, this tiny gland can cause weight and blood pressure to skyrocket and hormones and sleep patterns to go haywire. Other structures within the limbic system that are associated with emotional reaction are the **amygdalae** and **hippocampus.**

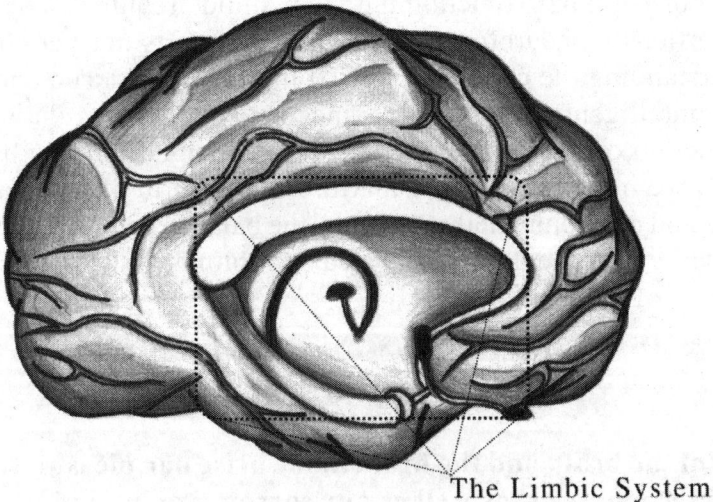

The Limbic System

Image 2: The Limbic System of the Brain

The Amygdalae:

The amygdalae are small almond-shaped regions found in both the left and right side of the brain which is involved in the formation and storage of memories associated with emotional events. This area of the brain generates many of the fear responses including immobility (frozen with fear); a rapid heartbeat and faster breathing, as well as the release of stress hormones. It is the bit of the brain that makes associations and sets off the body's alarms during an acute panic attack. Using MRI technology, neuroscientists have established that patients with depression, bipolar disorder or social phobia have exaggerated left amygdala activity and volume.

Scientists are beginning to unravel the complexity of the brain, but even so we are still many years away from truly understanding the connections between mental health and the changes that can be observed in brain structure and chemistry!

Recent fMRI (functional Magnetic Resonance Imaging) studies have shown that acupuncture stimulation has the ability to induce signal changes within the amygdalae. Researchers ran MRI scans of the brains on a group of individuals as they were undergoing acupuncture. The results showed that acupuncture had a powerful effect on the amygdala. Although the research study was designed to examine acupuncture's role in pain, it could explain acupuncture's effectiveness in treating both anxiety and depression. In the Chapter "Helpful Therapies", we will take a look at ways in which we can positively affect the areas of the brain that are affected by depression and anxiety.

Electrical circuits

The neurotransmitters that we discussed earlier (serotonin, dopamine, acetylcholine etc) help the nerves in sending tiny electrical signals between them. The nerves of the autonomic nervous system are a very vast network of electrical circuits which connects 40 trillion cells, and has a total length twelve times the circumference of the earth!

This amazing system electrically controls vital processes in the body that you hardly give a thought to, such as breathing, body temperature, metabolism, hormone function etc. It controls all of the numerous automatic processes without which you could not live. Virtually every cell in your body is connected to each other through the autonomic nervous system which controls much of their function.

So you can imagine that if something goes wrong with this electrical system, the symptoms would be widespread throughout your body!

Abnormal electric signals can result from infection, chemical or emotional trauma. In turn this signal is transmitted throughout the rest of your body via the autonomic nervous system, creating havoc! This is why mental anguish is often accompanied by physical symptoms throughout the bodies.

When it comes to anxiety, we are mainly concerned with two branches of the nervous system, the Sympathetic Nervous System (SNS) and the Parasympathetic Nervous System (PNS).

When you are relaxed, the Parasympathetic Nervous System (PNS) takes charge of all your body functions. The heart beats regularly, blood pressure is stable, inflammation is kept at bay, digestion functions smoothly, the mind is calm and relaxed, and the cells can repair and regenerate. In studies, activity has also been linked to feelings of security and safety. I have a colleague who calls this state "flowing with the waves".

However, when the Sympathetic Nervous System (SNS) takes control, the body goes into a state of fight or flight and the body's resources are channeled into "survival mode". All blood flow and energy is channeled into the heart and lungs, and glucose (which is usually stored in the liver) is released into the bloodstream. This mobilises the body enabling it to cope with the stress at hand. The heart races, the chest tightens, you feel the need to get out of the situation that you're in.

When the SNS is active, all non-essential functions in the body are put on hold, and energy is channeled away from these critical systems. The SNS is perfectly designed to help us cope with acute stress situations, but it is designed for fight or flight. When we're in situations where we cannot run or fight, or when the stress continues for a long time, several things happen:

1. During acute stress, large amounts of Noradrenalin are released into the bloodstream initially to mobilize the body and help it deal with stress. At first the changes are adaptive and they improve the individual's chances for survival (e.g. having enough energy and stamina to run away from danger). However, if the situation continues for some time, or you have a low stress

tolerance, the Noradrenalin levels become depleted. Several conditions are associated with low noradrenalin levels e.g. inability to cope with stress, chronic depression, anxiety, anorexia, Parkinson's disease and Alzheimer's disease.

2.   Levels of the stress hormone cortisol initially increase enlarging the adrenal glands – in which case symptoms such as high blood pressure and central obesity develop. In time cortisol levels become depleted (although the adrenal glands remain enlarged), leading to a variety of conditions such as anxiety, depression, chronic fatigue syndrome, fibromyalgia, chronic pelvic pain etc.

At this stage, the person is dealing not only with mental changes such as anxiety, depression or panic but may have physical changes that add to the stress on the system. Image 3 shows the effects on the body from being in either a PSN or SNS state.

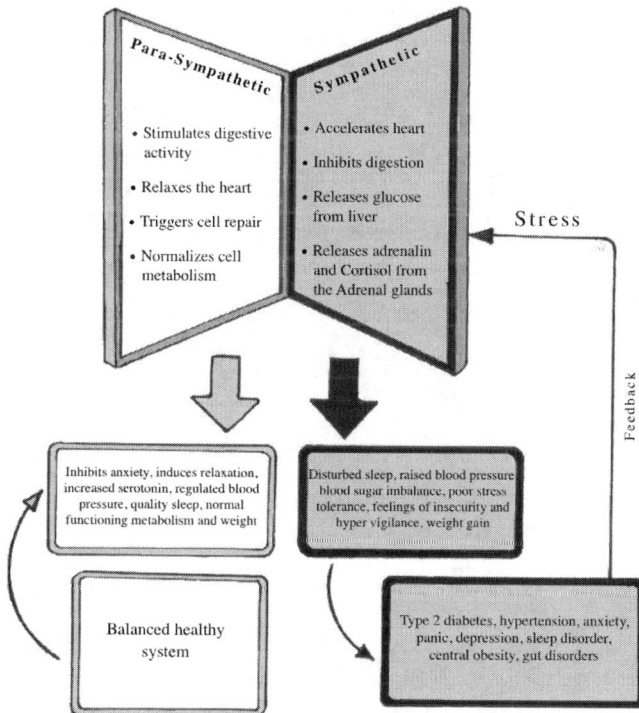

Image 3: The branches of the nervous system

In a chronic SNS state, the effects on the system such as raised blood pressure or disturbed sleep create a feedback loop adding fuel to an already stressed nervous system. Very often, this is the stage at which people would seek help, usually for their physical ailment, mentioning only in passing that they are affected by mental changes. Patients coming in for treatment are usually overly concerned about their gut disorder, weight gain or raised blood pressure and believe that these conditions are at the root of their anxiety or depression.

We must not only concern ourselves with treating the physical ailment, without also addressing the mind, emotions and the soul. Only in doing so can you fully resolve health conditions, rather than treat only symptoms of a larger problem. In the next chapter we will look at some of the common causes of anxiety, panic or depression.

CHAPTER 3

What may be causing my depression or anxiety?

In some cases, depression or anxiety is preceded by a specific life situation or event. Perhaps you've had a loss after which anxiety and depression naturally followed, but over time the condition has lingered. Often, however, these conditions come about for no obvious reason. Getting to the root of anxiety or depression can be tricky, but is absolutely essential to having a positive outcome as these conditions will recur if not addressed.

Each person is individual and often there is a very clear cause for the condition, but many times there isn't. More often than not, there is a complicated mixture of factors at play. In this section, we'll look at the different underlying factors which may be contributing to your mental health.

When we try to understand what may be the cause of depression or anxiety it is important to keep in mind that we are essentially made up of 3 parts; mind, body and soul. When all three are balanced and in good health the mind is clear, balanced, peaceful and calm. When one aspect is disturbed all 3 may be influenced. In other words, when the body or soul is out of balance, the mind will be unsettled, anxious or depressed. For instance, if there is a physical imbalance such as a thyroid condition its effects will be felt physically (tiredness), emotionally (depression) and mentally (poor concentration).

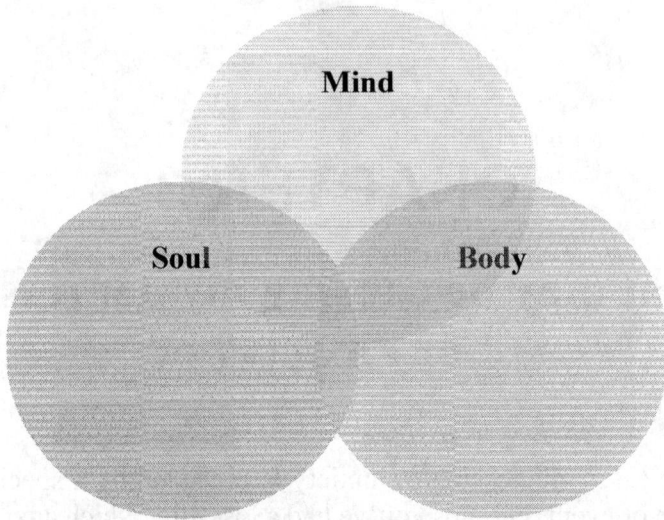

The Mind, body and soul connected

For this reason, treating only the mind with anti-depressants or anti-anxiety medication will help initially but it only masks a lurking problem. Holistic healing systems, such as Traditional Chinese Medicine focus on treating the entire person instead: mind, body and soul to regain mental health and balance; creating well-being without side-effects!

Also, it is now believed that for many individuals, a tendency towards anxiety and/or depression stems from early on in life. It is thought that stress or nutritional deficiencies during critical times of brain development of the fetus determine our "basal stress response" or our predisposition to mental imbalances. This basal stress baseline can be compared to a golf handicap. In other words, if you have a lower basal stress response you may be more vulnerable to stress, anxiety, depression or any mental health condition. Stress later on in life may affect you more acutely than it would for others. The following formula shows us how the basal stress response is determined. The basal stress response is the "starting point" from which we can calculate the individual's susceptibility to mental and emotional imbalances.

Genes + early adversity + nutrition + environment + trauma = basal stress response

Genes & early adversity

There is a known hereditary component to mood disorders. Studies involving twins demonstrate that identical twins (who have the same genetic fingerprint) have a considerably higher concurrence for mood disorders than non-identical twins. Family studies have shown that biological relatives of patients with depression are up to 3 times more likely to develop depression than the general population.

It has also long been known that early life adversities may influence our tendency to develop mental or physical disorders later in adulthood. It is now thought that prenatal or early postnatal events may critically alter central nervous system functioning. Stress occurring during critical times of the baby's brain development may alter the "programming" of the nervous system. In one interesting study, researchers were able to trace back the effects of early life stress on the genetic level in a group of rats. The rats that experienced early life stress had alterations in their genetic expression of stress patterns. These rats were showing a different genetic pattern from rats that were not stressed. They had "stress" wired into their genes!

This is not surprising as there is a mass of research showing that early stress, abuse or neglect alters the normal functioning of the nervous system. Nature may even have its reasons for doing so. Children born into high stress situations such as war tend to be more hyper-vigilant which does serve them well to be able to survive those conditions, but they do suffer the consequences mentally later on in life as they struggle with this handicap. Many of them will go on to develop a strong and healthy mental outlook, but always with heightened effort.

Dr. Hellhammer, the author of *Stress: The brain-body connection* believes that our mental predisposition is determined already in very early life. Many of us have then come into the world with an underlying susceptibility for depression and anxiety, either because of the genes we have inherited or our very early experiences. If our nutrition is good and no contributing health factors present, we remain mentally healthy. If, however, in the long run the other factors in the formula become compromised, one may well head straight into anxiety or depression. For instance, if you have a lowered basal stress response (or stress tolerance), a car accident or a serious virus may be enough to tip the balance and start an anxiety disorder.

I recently saw a patient who was suffering from severe panic disorder. It had all started the year before with a very minor car accident. In fact, her car had barely scathed another vehicle. She couldn't' understand how a very minor incident had triggered panic, something she had never experienced before. We started talking about her early life and she spoke about the stress her mother had experienced as a single mother, bringing her into this world alone. Her mother had been kicked out on the street when it became apparent that she was pregnant. Despite this, her mother had taken good care of her and had worked hard to raise her. She was not aware of any childhood stress and felt well taken care of, but her mother's stress during pregnancy would have impacted on her nervous system development. It took only a small incident to bring the whole nervous system to a state of panic. She has in the meantime recovered just by giving her body the needed nutritional support and a course of acupuncture to reduce the reactivity of the nervous system.

We have no control over our early lives, and if you have come into this world with a "stress handicap", you will have to pay even more attention to the other factors in the formula. Although your handicap may subtract from your basal stress response (stress tolerance), you can also "add" to your formula by managing nutrition, the environment, keeping body energy in balance by using therapies such as acupuncture etc.

If genes and early adversity contribute to our later mental health, should we then blame our parents for depression and anxiety? We could, but that would not help us in our healing process. And as long as we are apportioning blame to anyone else for our condition, whether it is parents, a partner, ex-partner etc. we take the control away from ourselves and create a block to the healing process. We need to accept responsibility for where we are at this point in life so that we can steer a way forward for healing. For genuine healing to take place, we have to accept our handicaps and rid ourselves of all blame and judgment so that we can see a way forward. For as long as we focus our energy on blaming others, our focus is on the "other" and we waste this precious resource (energy).

There is more about this in the section on Taking Responsibility. Knowing, however, that you have a "stress handicap" can help you to take better control of your life; empowering you to make healthier choices.

Nutrition

When I first began practicing in Scotland, I was astounded by the number of my patients who were taking prescription anti-depressants and/or anti-anxiety medication. In the East I would very seldom have a patient who had these on their prescription lists, but by the end of my first week consulting in Scotland, I had seen more than a dozen! I wondered whether Scottish doctors were over-prescribing these medicines, or were individuals here more prone to these conditions as compared to the patients I had seen in China and Singapore.

Culturally, in the East, people are more reluctant to acknowledge depression and anxiety, so my first thought was that people in Scotland were more likely to reach out for help. But I knew that as part of our training, we were able to spot signs of depression and anxiety in patients using traditional diagnoses (tongue, pulse, eyes, etc), and in fact we had been trained to pick up on this in a culture reluctant to talk about these issues. I knew then that I was seeing considerably more people with these conditions in Scotland, than I ever came across in the East.

I then researched and tried to understand this finding. From my research it soon became apparent that the only striking difference was what we are putting into our mouths! The patients I was seeing in the East were mostly on very basic, traditional diets, whereas patients in Scotland were in many cases consuming processed foods containing a complex mixture of chemicals!

Most people are unaware that their diets may be causing depression, phobias and anxiety. Brain neurotransmitters are, however, made from amino acids that must be obtained from the diet. Apart from the amino acids, certain vitamins and minerals are also required for the creation of the neurotransmitters. If the diet is deficient in nutrients, neurotransmitter deficiency develops. What is even more worrying though, is that certain processed foods actually disrupt the production of some of these vital neurotransmitters. I certainly know that if I've been eating the wrong foods, I become more prone to depression and anxiety. I was diagnosed many years ago with an inflammatory bowel condition at the time when I lived in Switzerland, and as a result I made several dietary changes. In time I also noticed that my depression and anxiety had almost vanished. When I went back to my old dietary patterns, the depression would hit back. I then began to realise the importance of diet, and how it affects the mental state. The first two of the 10 steps to breaking the cycle of anxiety and depression involve getting the right nutrition into the body. Optimizing the diet is crucial in treating both depression and anxiety, and so there will be more on this in the section "What's the Fix?".

Environment

In our modern world, the brain is constantly bombarded by sounds, rapid visual effects from television, movies, electronic monitors, radio waves, fluorescent artificial light, etc. This can at times be a huge amount of sensory bombardment for the brain to deal with, and can overwhelm the nervous system. If you are anxious by nature and find it difficult to sleep or relax, avoid watching television or sitting in front of a computer screen for at least an hour before bed, and try to avoid artificial light as much as possible (not easy over the winter months in Europe!).

The neurotransmitter Melatonin, which is involved in sleep patterns, is inhibited by light, and so making sure that the bedroom is dark at night is exceptionally important to those individuals who are affected by sleep disturbances.

Also within the environment, it may be necessary to determine your energy drains. These are situations, relationships, activities or people that leave you feeling down, low or anxious. The final step to achieving a healthy mind focuses on clearing energy drains and this is discussed in more detail in the Section "What's the fix?".

Stress/trauma

Stressful situations or traumatic events can lay down the foundation for anxiety and depression patterns to develop. It is well known that childhood abuse (sexual or emotional) is linked to adult depression. If this is the case, processing some of the emotions surrounding the abuse may be necessary in order to move on.

If, however, your current situation is causing your anxiety (financial, relationship, work, etc.), you may be able to change the situation. In fact, you must change the situation. Ignoring these stresses will eventually just snowball, leading to greater anxiety or depression until they are somehow tackled. If you're feeling overwhelmed by the thought of change, counseling can often be of great help. Even if you are not going down the formal counseling road, sometimes having a good friend as a sounding board can really be beneficial.

I remember once seeing a young woman in her twenties who had complete alopecia. She had lost every hair on her head and subsequently depression had set in. Hair loss can be extremely distressing to both men and women even when it is anticipated, for instance during cancer treatment. But in her case, she had unexplained alopecia, and her doctor had put it down to stress and had prescribed anti-depressants.

However, she told me that she felt that she wasn't stressed, as she had a non-stressful job and was comfortable financially, meditated, exercised and did "all the right things". I felt a completely different picture on the pulse though; her pulses were tight like a violin string. I tried to find other sources of stress in her life, and she eventually told me that she'd had an abortion two months before the alopecia had set in. Not wanting anyone to know, including her family, she went back to work 2 days after and never told a soul as she felt so ashamed of her decision to terminate the pregnancy. Her friends and family were unable to understand why she was avoiding them.

As she wept, she told me that this was the first time she had thought about what had happened as she had suppressed and blocked her emotions so much. She also was not able to face family and friends since the abortion, and had thus isolated herself. What was really important here was that she needed to acknowledge the pain that she had gone through. Because she had repressed her feelings and emotions, the body expressed the stress physically through her hair loss. We spoke about finding a way for her to reconnect with her family and friends. She was eventually able to confide in family and friends, and found comfort instead of the scorn she had anticipated. I'm happy to say that she has a full head of hair now and that her depression has lifted.

The case above once again highlights the balance between mind, body and spirit. It is often the case that if you suppress emotion, it will manifest in the physical. Thus, take note of your physical symptoms; they may be clues to what is going on mentally, emotionally and spiritually.

Gut imbalance: I've swallowed my brain!

In the past, medical science has separated each of the organs and their functions in an attempt to understand their function better. In doing so, we gained information about how organs functioned independently, but the intricate connections between organs and systems were overlooked. Many traditional healing systems have always expressed their concern about this reductionist approach (the approach to understanding the complex body by reducing it to the interaction of their parts).

However, developmental biology has opened up the opportunity to once again look at the connection between body parts. At first, scientists were puzzled as to why the gastrointestinal tract would produce and contain such a large amount of neurotransmitters. In fact, more than 90% of serotonin is found in the gut! Now we know that as the embryo develops in the womb, the brain and the gut (esophagus, stomach, small and large intestine) are created from the same cell lines. As the embryonic cells divide and separate, the cells develop into the different body structures. Some of the divisions are made very early on in the development separating into organs or structures; others remain intricately connected until later on the development. One line of cells that differentiates only later on in the development will eventually separate: one part growing into the central nervous system (the brain) and the other the enteric nervous system (the gut brain). The two are then connected by the vagus nerve.

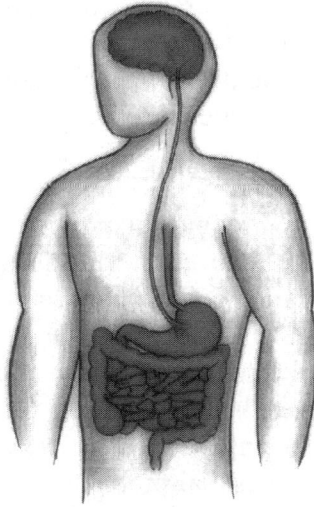

Image 4: the brain-gut connection

In essence what this means is that the cells in the proper brain and the cells in the gut are very similar in function. This is especially important when it comes to the production and use of neurotransmitters. It means that we cannot consider the brain in isolation. Whatever affects the brain also affects the gut. Traditional Chinese Medicine (TCM) has been aware of this connection for centuries and many mental health conditions in this system are treated primarily through the digestive organs. In Western medicine there is recognition of the connection between anxiety and bowel disturbances, and researchers are now beginning to realise the importance of this connection. However, it's probably more important to look at the flip side!

The gut's brain, the enteric nervous system, works very much like the proper brain. Researchers have shown that its nerve cells are influenced by the same neurotransmitters that we find in the brain. It contains very similar cells to those in the proper brain, together with complex circuitry that can zap messages between neurons. Just as the brain can upset the intestines, so can the intestines upset the brain.

This concept was first brought to the attention of the scientific world by a professor of anatomy and cell biology at Columbia University, Michael Gershon. The more he researched this connection, the more it became clear why people with gut disorders feel the way that they do. One example that most people can identify with is the "butterflies in the stomach: The stomach contains many sensory nerves that are stimulated when the brain is thinking anxious thoughts resulting in the "butterflies" feeling.

Fear, for instance, will cause the vagus nerve to increase its activity, resulting in diarrhea, choking or difficulty in swallowing. We're only just beginning to understand the connections, but if you think about this powerful connection what does this mean in terms of heartburn, IBS, constipation and diarrhea?

It's no surprise then, that medications that are developed to work on receptors in the brain would also have an effect on receptors in the gut. Dr. Gershon believes that this explains the side-effects of many anti-depressants. He explains that nearly a quarter of people on anti-depressants have gastrointestinal problems such as nausea, diarrhea and constipation. Also, anti-depressants may just be masking an underlying condition, and so I believe they should be used with utmost caution and only when all underlying conditions have been ruled out. Unfortunately, they are too easily prescribed before any investigations are undertaken to determine the cause of depression.

If your gut is not in good health, it will affect neurotransmitter levels in the brain! Now that means that it is necessary to treat gut conditions if there is to be any improvement in mental health! Very often, just treating a bowel condition can bring about big changes in depression and/or anxiety. In fact, in my training as an acupuncturist, we learned how the digestion and intestinal functions were at the root of creating a healthy mind. Only now are scientists beginning to understand what Chinese medicine has known for over 5000 years!

When I worked in China in the neurology unit, I was surprised how much emphasis was placed on gut health in these units. We know for instance that individuals who are victims of Alzheimer's and Parkinson's diseases usually suffer from constipation long before they get their diagnoses. The nerves in their gut are as affected as the nerve cells in their brains. In these cases, the gut also has to be treated to slow down the progression of these degenerative conditions. This would include congestive bowel toxicity, Candida/yeast overgrowth conditions, increased intestinal permeability (leaky gut syndrome) and conditions such as coeliac disease. In a traditional Chinese hospital, all of these would be addressed as a matter of priority in Parkinson's treatment.

One of my very dear patients who has Parkinson's has completely halted the progression of his condition now for more than 5 years without the use of medication, only by keeping to a very strict diet, and by making sure that his bowels are always functioning smoothly. In fact, one of his consultants has commented that he thinks (to his own surprise) that there has been an improvement and slight reversal of his condition.

Healthy bowel function is fundamental to a healthy functioning mind. A good friend of mine was being treated for schizophrenia until doctors discovered that she was, in fact, affected by coeliac disease. It took 6 months on the right diet to ease her symptoms, and she never had any signs of schizophrenia again until several years later when she went traveling and found it difficult to adhere to her diet. Within weeks she was institutionalized. She has been acutely aware of how diet influences her mental health but it was not until recently that research began into this area. A study in 2004 in Denmark showed that coeliac patients are 3 times more at risk for developing schizophrenia than those without the disease.

A young woman that I was treating had recently been diagnosed with Ulcerative Colitis and was undergoing surgery on her intestine. For years she was in a terrible emotional state and struggled with very severe anxiety, depression and obsessive thinking. A few weeks after the surgery, she came in to see me and it was hardly possible to recognise her. Surgery is a very radical treatment which no doubt had its detrimental effects, but after the diseased area in her intestine was removed, her obsessive thinking had died down and her mental health changed completely! She now recalls how extreme her anxiety had been when her gut had been ill and the connection in her mind is crystal clear.

The gut-brain connection concept is firmly ingrained in the ancient concepts of Traditional Chinese Medicine. The section "Traditional Chinese Medicine and Acupuncture" will explore anxiety and depression from a TCM perspective and will also focus on the gut connection.

Coeliac disease, inflammatory bowel disease, food intolerance, lactose intolerance, fructose malabsorption are some of the gut conditions I will touch on. This is by no means an exhaustive list and it is important to keep in mind that any gut condition could adversely affect the mind.

Coeliac disease

Coeliac disease is an intolerance to the protein in gluten, a substance found in wheat and other grains. For susceptible people, gluten injures the small intestinal lining and damages the fine structures (called "villi") that absorb nutrients. The resulting malnutrition, together with the by-products of gluten-metabolism, is what underlies mental disorders in many coeliacs. This condition highlights very clearly the brain-gut link.

Coeliac Disease

- Coeliac disease is a gluten intolerance
- Coeliac disease is linked to mental illness including ADHD, autism, depression and schizophrenia
- Strict gluten avoidance can resolve some mental health issues
- Common symptoms include weight loss and diarrhea, depression, anxiety and muscle

Recent successes with gluten-free therapy in mainstream medicine provide some indirect support for the connection of coeliac disease with mental illness. One study showed a strong link between coeliac disease and Attention Deficit Hyperactivity Disorder (ADHD). A Finnish study showed that patients with coeliac were more likely to have major depressive episodes, as well as disruptive behavioural disorders. With complete gluten avoidance, marked improvements were reported by a number of individuals with autism, depression and schizophrenia. A Hungarian study also showed complete resolution of neurological symptoms for coeliac patients on a strict gluten-free diet.

Many undiagnosed coeliacs have symptoms that mimic schizophrenia and other mental, psychological or emotional disorders. The good news is that coeliac disease, when identified early enough, is controlled with a very careful diet. Coeliac disease cannot be cured, but gluten-avoidance can make an enormous difference for these individuals. Coeliacs are advised to increase their intake of foods high in vitamin B, as well as omega oils, to heal the gut.

Earlier on, I described how a friend of mine had suffered from schizophrenia for years before it was determined that she had coeliac disease. Within a few months of starting a gluten free diet her mental heath was back to normal. Years later when she went travelling, she was unable to avoid gluten and very quickly her schizophrenia returned. These days she manages well and is emotionally very stable. For individuals like my friend, the connection between her gut health and mind is indisputable.

Often coeliac disease does not present with any symptoms at first. The most common symptoms include weight loss and diarrhea, depression, anxiety and muscle weakness. Up to 85% of patients with histologically proven coeliac disease have no gastrointestinal symptoms, so if you are suffering from any mental health concern, it is advisable to ask your GP for an antibody test for coeliacs. If you are diagnosed with coeliac disease, I would strongly recommend seeing a nutritionist who can help not only find suitable gluten substitutes, but also help replenish some of the critical nutrients that would have resulted from malabsorption.

Food intolerance

A food allergy is an adverse reaction to a particular food (e.g. nuts, shellfish) that involves the body's immune system. It can produce symptoms like rashes or it can be sudden and life-threatening (called analphylaxis), needing urgent medical attention. Food allergies affect just a few people.

Food intolerances, however, are more common. It happens when the digestive system is unable to process a certain type of food, the by-products of which then play havoc in the gut (recall how many neurotransmitters are produced in the gut!)

Although there could be an intolerance to almost any food, when it comes to chronic depression, wheat appears to be the major culprit. Sometimes the depressive effect of a food may be

Food Intolerance

- An inability of the body to metabolise a certain type of food
- Wheat products, for those who are sensitive, is a common culprit for depression
- Symptoms are wide ranging including digestive upset, mental lethargy, fatigue, depression, anxiety an fatigue.

cumulative rather than immediate. Sometimes the food may be eaten in moderation without causing any symptoms, but accumulated intake of the food may cause onset of depression and anxiety. In some people, the depressive effect may be immediate. Wheat is particularly known for producing this effect.

Symptoms of food intolerance are difficult to pinpoint and can be very vague including headaches, digestive upset, mental lethargy, depression, anxiety and fatigue.

Excluding wheat from the diet for a minimum of four weeks is the most effective way to diagnose this intolerance. For substitutes, try pasta or breads made from rye, rice and buckwheat or stick to wholegrain rice, quinoa or buckwheat.

Although wheat is the most common food intolerance linked to depression (and sometimes anxiety), any food can cause problems if the body is unable to metabolise it. I've had patients intolerant to olives or lemons, who have had similar experiences. I would suggest trying a wheat free diet for 3 weeks and if symptoms persist consider food intolerance testing. Food intolerances are easily tested and is a good place to start for anyone suffering from unexplained depression or anxiety accompanied by fatigue.

Lactose Intolerance

Almost all babies are born with the capacity to produce the enzyme lactase which enables them to break down the natural sugars in breast milk. As we grow, many of us will lose the ability to metabolise this sugar. Lactose intolerance is a condition where the body no longer produces the enzyme lactase, and as a result cannot break down lactose, the sugar found in milk. It is a surprisingly common condition affecting up to 15% of the British population.

These sugar molecules, if not broken down by the enzyme, tend to build up in the intestines. The intestinal bacteria waste no time in metabolizing the sugar themselves, leading to large-scale fermentation in the gut with copious amounts of gas being produced. People who are lactose intolerant suffer stomach cramps, bloating and flatulence; often even with trace amounts of dairy. The resulting damage to the intestine will lead to a reduced uptake of the amino acid tryptophan, the precursor of both serotonin and melatonin. The result: anxiety and depression.

Lactose Intolerance

- Individuals with lactose intolerance lack an enzyme to break down the natural sugar in milk
- Symptoms include flatulence, stomach cramps, bloating, flatulence, anxiety and depression
- Some people have only the mental symptoms and no gut symptoms
- Avoidance of dairy products is necessary to enable the absorption of the amino acid tryptophan, the precursor to serotonin and melatonin

Scientists are unsure as to why certain people become lactose intolerant but we do know that viral infections or genetics have a part to play. There have been several viruses thought to induce lactose intolerance. It may also be that losing the lactase enzyme may just be a natural part of maturation.

In nature, milk is reserved for the young. As animals grow they no longer need milk. There are many people who believe that humans are no different and that once we've weaned from the breast, the body no longer requires milk; especially not milk from another species. The milk industry may disagree and tout milk as being beneficial because of its calcium content. Most health practitioners would agree that the harmful effects of dairy outweigh the small amount of calcium it offers.

It is also interesting to note that while only 15% of the British population is thought to be lactose intolerant, 98% of Southeast Asians and 100% of native Americans do not produce the enzyme past childhood.

A small percentage of lactose intolerant individuals will not have the digestive symptoms, so don't rule lactose intolerance out if you don't have gut symptoms. I have seen many patients who's anxiety or even obsessive thinking improves dramatically when they cut out dairy. It is possible to get tested for lactose intolerance by your GP by undergoing a Hydrogen breath test whereby you fast overnight and are then given a drink of pure lactose. Blood tests to measure your sugar levels as well as monitoring how much hydrogen is in the breath, can confirm the diagnosis. However, it is probably much simpler to completely abstain from all dairy (even watch your supplements as they often contain lactose) for three weeks and then to drink a glass of milk. If you are lactose intolerant you will begin to feel unwell within a short period of time.

Fructose Malabsorption

Fructose is the natural sugar found in fruits. So that should be good for you, right? Well, there are a few individuals who struggle, just like with lactose, to break down fruit sugars. The most common symptoms of fructose malabsorption include bloating, flatulence, gurgling, abdominal pain and diarrhoea. Less frequently depression, anxiety, fatigue, headache, brain fog, craving for sugar, and weight loss are also present. Once again, the symptoms of depression and anxiety are the result of changes in the gut which prevent the absorption of the building blocks required to make the feel good neurotransmitters. In particular, individuals affected by fructose malabsorption tend to have lower levels of the amino acid tryptophan.

Fructose Malabsorption
▪ The body's inability to metabolise the natural sugar in fruit (fructose)
▪ Symptoms include bloating, flatulence, abdominal pain, anxiety, fatigue, headache, sugar cravings and brain fog
▪ A reduction in the consumption of fructose is needed

I remember once seeing a young student, David, who was very health conscious. He was doing everything right, yet he continued to have chronic gut problems, fatigue and concentration problems. He was frustrated as he watched his friends gurgling down beer and fries and they seemed healthy enough to study, party and play sport. Whereas he was eating all the right foods, avoiding everything deemed unhealthy and there he was, too tired and ill most of the time to participate in sport. His studies were also affected as he struggled to concentrate. In time, depression and anxiety grew. Looking at his diet, he was having fruit for breakfast, as well as in between meals for snacks, and was eating health bars which contained high fructose. For most people, this would be a healthy choice, but for someone with fructose malabsorption, they are like poison apples. David found it difficult to give up fruit as an experiment as he felt they were important for his health, but he agreed to try low fructose fruits for a few weeks. The change was astounding!

There is rising concern about the growing popularity of high fructose products, especially in a society where sugar has received bad press. Many processed products contain high fructose levels, marked on food labels as food juice concentrates or corn syrup. Many health products have removed glucose and have replaced them with natural fruit sugars, and although they are healthier for most people, they cause problems for individuals with fructose malabsorption.

There is also a lot of misconception about the sugar content in fruit. A common belief is fruits contain mainly, or only, fructose sugar. Many fruits, however, contain an equal amount of fructose and glucose. Some common fruits contain considerably higher fructose than glucose, these high fructose fruits include apple, pear, and watermelon, which have over twice as much fructose as glucose. So for most people, but not all, the saying "an apple a day keeps the doctor away" rings true.

Now, I can hear some of you thinking "Oh for goodness sake! They keep changing their minds about what is good and bad". That is true. On one day you will find an article saying that scientists have found a certain food to be good for one thing, and then the next you're told to avoid it for another reason. Many people have become so confused about foods and what they should be eating but it certainly makes the point that we are individuals. For most of the population, apples are a good thing, but for the few who are fructose malabsorbers, they will cause trouble.

It is essential to keep in mind that we are individuals and your healing path will be a unique journey. It is not always easy at first to see what the underlying cause of your depression and anxiety may be, but it may be that missing ingredient that holds the key to permanently resolving the issue.

Back to fructose malabsorption; The common symptoms include: bloating, flatulence, gurgling, abdominal pain, diarrhea, depression, anxiety, fatigue, headache, brain fog and cravings for sugar. Consider taking fructose out of the diet for two weeks if you regularly suffer from the symptoms above to see if your condition improves.

Foods with a high fructose content to avoid:

- Apple, pear, melon, papaya, quince, star fruit, watermelon, coconut
- Dried fruits
- Honey
- Sugar substitutes such as agave syrup, xylitol, sorbitol or Fructose Oligosaccharides (FOS)
- Fruit juices and fruit juice concentrates
- Fruit pastes - chutney, relish, plum sauce, sweet & sour sauce, BBQ sauce.
- Fortified wines
- High Fructose Corn Syrup - many processed products including soda drinks contain this
- Corn syrup

Fruits with lower fructose (than glucose) can be consumed in small amounts:

- apricot, nectarine, peach, plum, grapefruit, lemon, lime, orange, banana, pineapple
- blueberry, blackberry, boysenberry, cranberry, raspberry, strawberry, loganberry

Tryptophan deficiency

Low levels of the feel good neurotransmitter, serotonin, can be responsible for depression and other psychological disturbances, such as anxiety, insomnia, fatigue, carbohydrate cravings, weight gain, poor concentration and low self-esteem.

Tryptophan is the precursor for both Serotonin and the sleep-inducing neurotransmitter Melatonin. Depression that is accompanied by sleep disturbance can often point towards a tryptophan deficiency.

There are two ways to rectify Serotonin Deficiency Syndrome. One method is through the natural method of increasing tryptophan intake and the other through the use of anti-depressants known as selective serotonin reuptake inhibitors (SSRIs) such as Prozac. SSRIs work by concentrating existing levels of serotonin in the brain, so they stay in the synapse between nerves and facilitate communication. They do not create serotonin, as many people believe, but simply collect the existing serotonin so it is used more effectively. Some studies suggest that long term use of SSRI anti-depressants actually reduce serotonin levels.

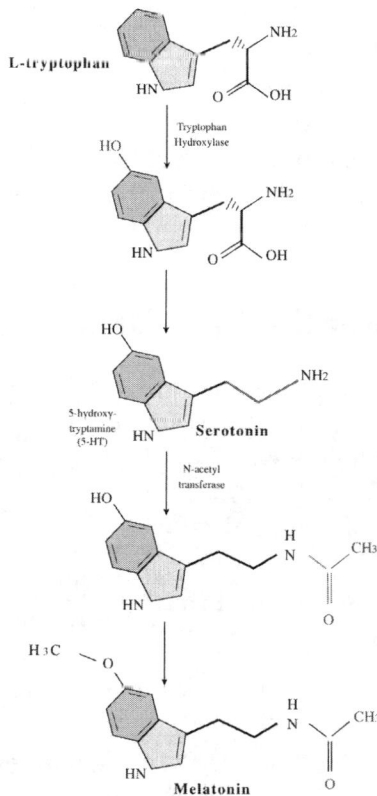

Image 5: the production of melatonin and serotonin from tryptophan

> **Tryptophan Deficiency**
>
> - A deficiency of the amino acid Tryptophan leads to insufficient production of serotonin and melatonin
> - Anxiety, depression, low moods and sleep disturbances, poor concentration and weight gain are common symptoms
> - Include foods such as sesame seeds, chickpeas, dark chocolate, oats, sunflower seeds and turkey

Some of the more serious side effects of these anti-depressants include heart palpitations, chest pain, decreased libido, suicide, nervous system disorders and tinnitus. Also, I am a strong believer in addressing the cause of the depression and/or anxiety rather than just masking the symptoms.

Good sources of tryptophan include sesame, fish, chickpeas, chocolate (make sure its pure dark chocolate), oats, sunflower seeds and turkey. If you are eating plenty of the foods that contain tryptophan but still experience depression, you may need to look at whether you have lactose or fructose intolerance. Both these conditions contribute to a deficiency of tryptophan even when there is a sufficient intake of the amino acid.

Essential Fats Deficiency

Some oils are essential to the body, and a deficiency in oils can

> **Essential Fats Deficiency**
>
> - A deficiency of essential fats can lead to difficulty learning, concentration issues as well as depression and fatigue.
> - Other conditions linked to essential fats deficiency include arthritis, high blood pressure, pre-menstrual tension & dry skin.

lead to a variety of mental-emotional symptoms. Just like an engine will need oiling, the brain too requires healthy oils to function. Fats are important for your body because they insulate the nerve cells, balance hormones, lubricate your joints as well as the brain! Depression, dyslexia, Attention Deficit Disorder

(ADD), fatigue, memory problems, difficulty learning may all be caused by an underlying deficiency of fatty acids. The amount and type of fats that we consume are very important. I find that patients are often very confused about which oils are good and which are bad. Generally the rule is that fats should be liquid. Fats that are hard (saturated fats) at room temperature, such as butter or the fat in meat, cause our systems to clog up. Fats that are liquid, such as olive or fish oils, provide the necessary nutrition for body and brain. Fish, especially cold water fishes, should be consumed at least twice a week, rather than fatty meats. Avoid fried foods and foods that are baked with solid oils such as butter. Liberally use olive oil, flaxseed oil, avocado oil on salads or cooked foods. For cooking, use olive or sunflower oil. Avoid cooking with butter.

Copper/Zinc imbalance

One of the most common trace-metal imbalances we find in today's world is elevated copper and deficient zinc. These trace elements act as neurotransmitters in the brain and both of them have an important physiological role to play but they don't play well together. Copper and zinc compete with one another for absorption in the gut and as copper levels increase, zinc becomes depleted. Recently, with more contamination, elevated copper levels are resulting in zinc deficiencies. An imbalance of these neurotransmitters has been associated with hyperactivity, attention deficit disorders, behavior disorders, anxiety and depression. Also, many of those labeled with autism

Copper/Zinc Imbalance
▪ Patients have elevated copper levels and lowered zinc
▪ Symptoms include: hyperactivity, ADD, anxiety, depression, acne, eczema, headaches, chronic sinus infections, insomnia, poor immune function
▪ White spot on nails may be a sign of zinc deficiency as a result of excess copper
▪ A history of Ulcerative Colitis increases the likelihood of a copper/zinc imbalance

and paranoid schizophrenia have elevated blood copper levels as well as other biochemical imbalances.

Individuals with high-copper levels often experience severe PMS and may have a family history of postpartum depression. This group also has a high incidence of acne, eczema, sensitive skin, tendency to easily sunburn, headaches, chronic sinus, post-nasal drip, poor immune function, insomnia and white spots on their finger nails. Joint and muscle pains are also often reported.

Patients with ulcerative colitis are more likely to absorb excess copper in their intestinal tissues which can lead to intestinal disorders, impaired healing and reduced resistance to infections. Hair analysis is the best method to detect copper imbalances.

Metabolic Imbalance

When the normal metabolic processes are disturbed, very often, the resulting shortfall or absence of a normal metabolite causes disturbance which can reverberate onto the mental level.

Histadelia

Histadelia
<ul><li>Results because of the body's inability to break down histamine</li><li>Condition is more common in males</li><li>Symptoms include: obsessive and compulsive thinking, phobias, chronic depression, hyperactivity, blank mind episodes, low pain tolerance, poor tolerance of heat, poor immune function, nausea, excessive saliva in the mouth, joint pain, muscle pain, headache and insomnia</li><li>Histadelics have slender fingers and toes</li><li>Has strong links to schizophrenia</li></ul>

Histamine plays an important role in sleep, immune and gut function. Although this protein is needed in small amounts for many normal body functions, excess histamine can cause problems. Chronically elevated histamine levels, in some cases, may be due to a metabolic imbalance that results from the body's inability to break down this protein. Called Histadelia, this condition can underlie a chronic depression and also mimics symptoms of Obsessive Compulsive Disorder (OCD). Symptoms include hyperactivity, compulsions, obsessions, addictive tendencies, blank mind episodes, phobias, chronic depression and strong suicidal tendencies. Physical signs can include little tolerance for pain, rapid metabolism, lean build, profuse sweating, seasonal allergies, good tolerance of cold and poor tolerance of heat, frequent colds, frequent unexplained nausea, excessive saliva in the mouth, phobias, joint pain or swelling, addictive tendencies, muscle pain, headache and insomnia.

These individuals are highly motivated perfectionists that work to the point of compulsion. Histadelics usually have slender fingers/toes rather than stubby fingers and toes. More than 15% of patients with schizophrenia also have Histadelia. A simple blood test can give information about a persons histamine levels. Histadelia is treated by supplementing the amino acid Methionine, which helps in the breakdown of histamine. In addition, a low protein and high complex carbohydrate diet is recommended.

Hypoglycemia

Another common condition that can cause anxiety and mood swings involves a metabolic error in sugar regulation. In most cases this is a reversible condition (and not a disease) which can be easily managed. If the body struggles to get the balance right, sugar levels in the blood may drop too low or too quickly. Most cells have small storage of glucose, and can use other forms of energy, but for nerve and brain cells glucose is their only form of energy. When there is not enough glucose available it rapidly affects the nervous system, shutting down vital functions.

After eating, the body releases the hormone insulin which enable the muscles, liver and tissues to take up glucose and store it. However, if the body is over-responding, producing too

Hypoglycemia
▪ Low blood sugar levels due to excessive insulin release
▪ Symptoms include: tremor, dizziness, nausea, goose bump skin, headaches, sweating, anxiety, irritability, lightheadedness and disorientation

much insulin then as a result, about 2 hours later, the body has stored all the glucose and nothing remains in the blood. The body registers low blood sugar levels and triggers an emergency, thereby dumping adrenalin into the blood stream triggering fear and panic. The brain becomes starved of fuel as there is no glucose available and at the same time the body is flooded with stress hormones leading to irrational thinking, nervousness, panic attacks, irritability and a roller-coaster of emotions!

If you regularly experience any of the following symptoms which worsen if you have not eaten for a few hours, hypoglycemia should be investigated: tremor, dizziness, nausea, goose bump skin, headaches, sweating, anxiety, irritability, lightheadedness and disorientation. Stabilising the blood sugar levels can bring not only relief from anxiety and panic attacks, but also emotional balance.

Inadequate exposure to sunlight

Most of us will feel seasonal changes and are very aware of the seasonal changes that happen especially around winter when the days get shorter and darker. I see the changes that happen in some of my patients too. Most people report more tiredness and typical "winter blues". But for others, Seasonal Affective Disorder (SAD) is a serious condition where people they experience depressive symptoms accompanied by changes in sleeping and eating patterns.

Inadequate sun exposure
• Lack of sunlight creates disturbances in the secretion of Melatonin
• Symptoms include depression, disturbed sleeping and eating patterns
• Get outdoors as much as possible during winter
• A medical lamp may be necessary to suppress Melatonin production
• Supplementation with vitamin D may also be required

Researchers believe that SAD relates to an imbalance of serotonin and melatonin. Melatonin, the hormone that regulates our sleep clocks, is suppressed by natural light. It is released in greater amounts in the darker nights, generally causing us to feel down and sleepy. It is thought that for those individuals sensitive to the effects of Melatonin, depression and sleep disturbances can set in. What can I suggest about this? Only to get outdoors and get as much of the little available sunlight during winter! For some people, SAD lamps are the only way to realistically keep serotonin levels up and melatonin production down during the winter months. These medical lamps are available without prescription, and may be recommended if your depression is seasonal. vitamin D supplementation is usually recommended throughout the year.

Hormonal changes

Hormonal changes affect both men and women in many ways. In fact, our hormone levels very often drive our behaviour and affect our moods. This section will cover the male and female sex hormones, as well as the stress hormone cortisol. Hormones have their effects throughout the body. Just like the neurotransmitters, they act as messengers in the body to regulate various functions within the body, mind and emotions.

Male Hormones:

Male Hormone Imbalance
<ul><li>A deficiency of testosterone leads to low libido, forgetfulness, sleep disturbance, low stamina, lack of motivation, fatigue and depression</li><li>Excessive testosterone may lead to aggression, risk-taking behaviour, irritability, anxiety and nervousness.</li><li>Zinc deficiencies may lead to lowered testosterone levels</li><li>Progesterone deficiency in men includes the low testosterone symptoms as well as memory and concentration problems, feeling spaced out or unreal, anxiety, irrational fears, mood swings, hypoglycemia and cold hands and feet.</li></ul>

When we think of male hormones, most of us will think of testosterone. While testosterone is one of the major male hormones, oestrogen and progesterone also play a discernable role in the male body. When it comes to hormones, it is all about finding the right balance. Each of the hormones have their important functions within the body, but they need to be produced in just the right ratios. A lack in testosterone, for instance, will lead to side effects such as low libido, forgetfulness, sleep disturbance, fatigue and depression. An excess of this same hormone could lead to aggression, irritability, anxiety, risk taking behaviour and nervousness. Somewhere in the middle of this continuum exists a calm, composed, motivated man (with lots of stamina). As you will see if you continue to read, the other hormones, such as oestrogen and progesterone, play equally an important role in both the physical and mental health. First, let us look at testosterone.

Testosterone:

The testes, and to a lesser extent the adrenal glands, are responsible for producing testosterone in men. It is considered the hormone of manhood as its responsible for male characteristics such as beard growth, deepening of the voice, energy production, producing muscle mass, growth of the Adams apple, enlarging the phallus and maturing of the sex organs. Sounds good so far, but testosterone is also important in mental health and maintaining cognitive functions as well as regulating the fight-or-flight response. Researchers from the University of Texas found that men with higher testosterone levels displayed more dominant, competitive behaviours and were more status driven than those with lower levels of the hormone. In fact, researchers were able to predict, just from testosterone levels what status these men wished to hold in society. Therefore, apart from all its physical functions, testosterone gives men their drive, competitive edge, quickness of mind and cool composure; as long as it falls within the right range.

Imbalances in testosterone levels can dramatically affect energy, mood and behaviour. Low testosterone levels can seriously dent a man's ego when he lacks libido and energy, feels depressed and lacks motivation. With low testosterone levels, these men wish to hide away from the world, remove themselves from competitive situations even when they have the ability to succeed.

With age, testosterone naturally declines, and some men over 40 may complain of reduced sex drive, loss of muscle mass and mood changes. Contributing to this natural decline, nutritional deficiencies, and in particular the element zinc, may lead to significantly low testosterone levels. When zinc levels are inadequate, testosterone levels drop leading to depression, a loss of stamina, fatigue and lack of motivation.

Men who are zinc deficient often just need to increase their zinc intake to restore testosterone levels. Foods that are rich in zinc include oysters, shellfish, chicken, beef, lamb, eggs, brown rice, oatmeal, cashews and green leafy vegetables. For others, it may take some skill in rebalancing the hormones.

There are many misconceptions about progesterone. It is often perceived as a female sex hormone. However, progesterone is a vital hormone in the body of both men and women for many general functions. It has a critical function of keeping the endocrine system balanced and is considered the "mother" of all hormones because it is the precursor to many important components (including oestrogen and testosterone). For men, a progesterone deficiency results in many of the low testosterone symptoms such as low moods, lack of libido and fatigue but in addition there will be memory and concentration problems, feeling unreal or spaced out, anxiety, irrational fears, hypoglycaemia, mood swings and cold hands and feet. It is amazing what a little hormone balance can do for men. Geoff, a 38 year old man was diagnosed with Chronic Fatigue Syndrome (CFS) the year before he came to see me. He complained not only of debilitating fatigue, but also of a wide range of cognitive symptoms. Geoff explained that he often felt spaced out or unreal. He was also plagued by chronic anxiety and tension, although on the surface he appeared calm. His major concern was lack of libido so we sent away samples for hormone testing. Geoff's results showed low progesterone and testosterone. We decided to try a small dosage of natural progesterone initially, and within two months, most of Geoff's symptoms had cleared up, including his chronic fatigue.

Female Hormones

Women tend to suffer more easily from depression and anxiety and it's not surprising as our hormone functions are a little more complicated than men's. I always recommend that women keep a daily diary of their symptoms numbered with the days of their menstrual cycle. If there is a correlation between bouts of anxiety and depression and your hormonal cycle, hormone testing may be necessary. Progesterone is often implicated in anxiety with low levels of this hormone being linked to heightened anxiety and depression. However, low oestrogen levels are also blamed for anxiety, depression and panic attacks and it may be difficult to guess what the hormonal mixture is just based on symptoms. If a hormonal imbalance is suspected, I always recommend getting a hormone rhythm test done over a period of a month to see the relative balance between the hormones.

	Progesterone	**Oestrogen**
Imbalance symptoms	• Loss of bone density • Imbalances of Zinc and copper • Blood sugar imbalance • Hormonal cancers • Depression • Anxiety • Migraine • Thyroid instability • Sleep disturbance	• Depression • Panic attacks • Low self esteem • Headaches • Vaginal dryness • Fatigue • Hot flashes • Difficulty concentrating • Memory problems • Skin dryness

Both Oestrogen and Progesterone play a significant role in women's mental health. This is seen very often just after childbirth and also at menopause and is the cause of postnatal depression and low moods during menopause.

Times when hormones are changing, such as puberty or menopause, can also bring about severe cases of anxiety and depression. Many women report changes in their level of anxiety and feel as if someone else has moved into their skin! Anxiety during menopause is extremely common as the hormones dance around, and while for some women it can be a slow dance, for others it's a crazy salsa! I see many very stressed menopausal women who are severely affected mentally and physically by the changes. The most important thing to keep in mind is that eventually (as the hormones find their new balance) the anxiety will pass. I would recommend testing the

Progesterone:Oestrogen ratio to determine whether there is an imbalance of these vital hormones. Based on the results, natural hormone boosters can be used. In the meantime, follow the dietary recommendations in this book, and make sure that you're getting enough exercise. Valerian and passion flower are good natural remedies that can help to ease menopause related anxiety. If depression is present Black Cohosh may be recommended.

Cortisol:

Cortisol is another hormone that is often implicated in depression. Individuals who are clinically depressed tend to have an excess of cortisol as compared to non-depressed individuals. Cortisol is secreted by the adrenal glands, which assist us in our reactions to stressful events.

Cortisol may continue to be secreted even though a person already has high levels in his or her blood leading to depression, hypertension, weight gain and ultimately diabetes. This hormone is believed to be related to clinical depression since the high levels usually reduce to a normal level once the depression disappears. It is also found that people with depression often release cortisol in an irregular pattern. I have found that, without exception, all of my patients with anxiety or depression have an altered cortisol pattern.

If this chronic secretion of cortisol continues for a long period of time, the adrenal glands become depleted and the cortisol output decreases. Low cortisol is also linked to depression and anxiety but is usually seen in patients displaying Fibromyalgia, irritable bowel syndrome, low back pain, inflammation, chronic fatigue syndrome or auto-immune conditions such as Rheumatoid Arthritis.

Underlying health conditions

Thyroid Imbalance

The thyroid gland sits in the neck just below the Adam's apple and is involved in controlling the metabolism; how quickly the body burns energy and makes proteins. It has another critical function, however, and that is to control how sensitive the body should be to the other hormones. It is because of its ability to make the body cells either hyper-sensitive or insensitive to the other hormones that widespread hormonal disruptions take place when this gland is out of kilter. The thyroid gland could be either overactive or under-active in its production of thyroid hormone.

When thinking about thyroid imbalance, one very remarkable case comes to mind. Jenny, a woman in her 50s had developed a tremor, agitation and anxiety after a few years of continuous stress. In the course of treatment, I measured her resting heart rate and was taken aback by the rapidness of the pulse. I checked it a few times and her pulse was consistently close to a 100. The Resonance Biofeedback session indicated that Jenny may have thyroid toxicity so I asked her to get a test done at her GP. She was then diagnosed with hyperthyroidism as a result of Grave's disease. This explained the anxiety and agitation.

Thyroid Imbalance

- This gland controls metabolism and the body's sensitivity to other hormones
- Symptoms of an underactive thyroid: weight gain, fatigue, depression, low-level anxiety, lack of motivation, dry skin, sluggish bowels and the tendency to have cold hands and feet. There is a tendency with an under-active thyroid to feel sluggish and tired
- Symptoms of an overactive thyroid: racing pulse, irritability, extreme anxiety, panic attacks, difficulty sitting still, hot flushes, loose bowels, trembling, thinning hair, depression and mood swings.

Jenny was then placed on medication by her doctor to suppress the thyroid, but through a treatment error, the thyroid was over-suppressed to the point where her thyroid became critically under-active. Jenny then began to feel depressed and unmotivated and struggled to come into the clinic just to keep her appointments. Once we realised what was going on, Jenny went off to her consultant who then prescribed synthetic thyroid replacement. With one drug "killing" the thyroid, and the other replacing the hormones, Jenny was on a roller coaster of depression, irritation, anger and weepiness. In time Jenny's thyroid balanced out and she was back to her usual self, but it really struck me how vital the thyroid balance is in both anxiety and depression. I myself was diagnosed with an under-active thyroid, and can empathize with the severe depression and anxiety that can accompany this thyroid state. Once when I was overdosed with thyroid hormone, I experienced the opposite spectrum - extreme agitation! After I had experienced these extremes, I was able to understand that we are in fact just chemical machines!

Symptoms of an under active thyroid include difficulty losing weight, fatigue, depression and low-level anxiety, lack of motivation, dry skin, sluggish bowels and the tendency to have cold hands and feet. There is a tendency with an under-active thyroid to feel sluggish and tired.

An overactive thyroid on the other hand gives a racing pulse, irritability, extreme anxiety, panic attacks, difficulty sitting still, hot flushes, loose bowels, trembling, thinning hair, depression and mood swings.

One way to get an idea whether the thyroid gland may need testing is through measuring the Basal Body Temperature (BBT) (see box). An early morning waking temperature can tell a lot about how your basal metabolism works, which may point to an under or over-active thyroid. The BBT temperature refers to a 'resting' or 'base' temperature. That means that your BBT *must* be measured prior to *any* physical activity, after at least three to four hours of sleep.

Measuring Your BBT Temperature

Measure your BBT temperature first thing each morning, as soon as you wake up. It is recommended that you remain in bed (as any physical activity can increase your resting temperature), as well as avoid eating or drinking. Insert the thermometer either into your mouth or ear. Read the temperature and record the reading. Do this for a minimum of 3 consecutive days (or longer if you would like to be more thorough). If you are a pre-menopausal woman you need to chart starting on the first day of your menstrual cycle as the hormone changes that occur throughout the month will also affect the readings. A normal reading is between 36.4 to 36.8°C. If your temperature is consistently falling outside of this range, thyroid testing is indicated.

Homocysteine and depression

Homocysteine is a naturally-occurring amino acid in the body which is rapidly converted to harmless substances by enzymes. These enzymes require vitamins B6, B12 and folic acid to work properly and if there are deficiencies in any of these, homocysteine levels rise. Your doctor will be aware that a high homocysteine level in the blood is a risk factor for many disease states, including cardiovascular disease, atherosclerosis, Alzheimer's disease and osteoporosis. Most doctors are, however, not aware of the link between homocysteine and depression.

Max, a 62 year old male had a history of heart problems, he also now complained of fatigue and low moods although he insisted that he was not depressed. Max had been very active in the past, a keen cyclist, but now his extreme fatigue and low moods prevented him from exercising. Because of his heart history, I decided to check out his vitamin B and homocysteine status. The laboratory report came back indicating very low vitamin B12 levels and not surprising, raised homocysteine. After 2 months of vitamin B12 injections Max was a different person entirely! With more energy on hand he was back to his usual cycling but more than that he noticed a significant improvement in his moods. Looking back, Max could see that he had been suffering from depression.

In a Rotterdam study of 3883 elderly individuals, researchers found a correlation between depression and low levels of folate,

Homocysteine

- Homocysteine is a naturally occurring amino acid which requires vitamin B6, B12 and folic acid to break it down
- Deficiencies of these vitamins cause homocysteine to build up
- Excess homocysteine linked to cardiovascular disease, atherosclerosis, Alzheimer's disease, osteoporosis and depression
- Raised homocysteine levels are often found with no other symptoms than depression initially

vitamin B12 and high levels of homocysteine. It is thought that normal homocysteine metabolism is necessary for the production of the neurotransmitters serotonin and dopamine.

It would appear that some individuals appear to require increased amounts of these vitamins to reduce their homocysteine levels. It is believed that this may be genetically determined, although this process becomes naturally less efficient with age. Supplementation may be necessary to bring the homocysteine levels back into the normal range. It is also known that patients with high homocysteine levels often do not respond well to antidepressant treatment. I wish that there was a symptom checklist that I could provide in this book, but homocysteine is unfortunately a silent killer. I recommend that everyone over the age of 40 should have their homocysteine levels checked, especially if there is a history of heart disease in your family.

Addictions

Addictions involve excessive dependence on any substance, including drugs, alcohol, cigarettes, work, sex or food. Addictions are usually characterized by the body or mind depending on the substance for normal functioning. There are many scientific theories as to how addictions occur chemically within the brain, but we do know that there is a strong relationship between GABA, dopamine and serotonin interactions with addictions.

You may wonder why addictions are discussed under the

Addictions
▪ Involves excessive dependence on substances such as drugs, alcohol, cigarettes, work, sex or food
▪ Addictions and mental health imbalances go hand in hand
▪ Addictions are caused by, but also lead to neurotransmitter imbalances
▪ Acupuncture is a very effective way of treating addictions by normalizing the reward cascade in the brain
▪ Acupuncture also reduces cravings and deals with withdrawal symptoms

heading of what may be causing your depression and/or anxiety. Doctors know that addictions and mental health problems go hand in hand. Very often individuals begin to use substances in response to depression, in an attempt to cope with emotional pain. In other cases, a pre-existing substance abuse precedes depression, especially with substances such as alcohol or cocaine. Whether it was the addiction that started first, or the depression and/or anxiety, the addictions need to be dealt with before you can truly be free of depression and anxiety. Addictions, because of the dysfunction they create in dopamine and serotonin metabolism, will in the long run cause our mental health to suffer.

Acupuncture is used world wide to treat addictions and has been extensively researched. By increasing serotonin in the hypothalamus region of the brain, acupuncture may help to normalize the complex functioning of the reward cascade. Addicts treated with acupuncture, not only experience a reduction of withdrawal symptoms, but also a reduction of the craving for the substance. When the reward cascade is functioning normally, the patient feels a sense of peace and wellbeing that lasts beyond the detoxification treatment. Acupuncture may thus be used not only during the withdrawal period, but also to prevent relapse.

Reactive Depression

When life incidents, such as loss, are the start of your depression it is important to remember that your emotions are a natural response to what has taken place. Depression and/or anxiety are natural responses after the loss of a loved one either through death or separation or with any other loss (e.g. financial). The only healer for these emotions is time and acknowledgement. Allowing yourself the time to grieve and acknowledging that the pain you experience is a necessary part of the emotional healing. Often keeping a journal in which you write down all your thoughts surrounding the loss and its effect on you can be healing in itself. If however, you continue to dwell on the loss it may be worth speaking to a counsellor.

There are many contributing factors to anxiety and depression and for some of you it will be clear at this point what may be causing your condition. Others may feel daunted by the large number of possibilities that have been offered. Over the past year, I have put together a questionnaire which contains more than 150 questions which will highlight possible areas of concern for you. The questionnaire, which can be found online at www.acuhealthuk.com, uses simple algorithms to determine your probability for conditions that may be contributing to your depression or anxiety. This includes vitamin deficiencies, underlying health conditions as well as Traditional Chinese Medicine patterns.

Once specific areas of concern are highlighted, it is then possible to narrow down the likely causes of anxiety and depression.

CHAPTER 4

Medications are not always the answer

If you have depression, you have most likely been offered an anti-depressant to reduce the symptoms. Anti-depressants work by concentrating the amount of the feel-good neurotransmitter, Serotonin, in the brain. Although effective to some degree in reducing symptoms, in the long run depression medications can actually make the underlying neurotransmitter deficiency worse. For example, if you have depressive symptoms caused by low levels of serotonin, taking a "SSRI" medication such as paroxetine, fluoxetine or citalopram is merely tricking the brain into thinking that it has more serotonin. These medications do not stimulate the production of more neurotransmitters. In fact, there is solid scientific evidence that they accelerate the depletion of the neurotransmitters over time. This is why many of these medications only work for a short time and then stop being effective.

In addition, the side effects such as headaches, fatigue and nausea to name just a few, can sometimes make long-term therapy with anti-depressants almost impossible to bear. The use of the anti-depressant Paroxetine has been associated with abdominal weight gain. Fluoxetine, another commonly prescribed anti-depressant is associated with both abdominal obesity and hypercholesterolemia. It is therefore strongly recommend that patients taking SSRIs be carefully monitored for obesity and elevated lipids in the blood. Paroxetine is highly addictive and withdrawal symptoms can be severe. According to the British Medical Journal, the manufacturer GlaxoSmithKline, has been forced to admit the very severe withdrawal symptoms that accompany this drug. In several patients I have witnessed withdrawal with very extreme obsessive thinking, agitation, panic and sleep disruptions. In fact, I have had patients who feel that they have to remain on this drug for life because withdrawal creates such extreme and violent reactions. In many cases withdrawal can continue for up to two years after discontinuing the drug.

At the time of writing this, there is yet another story in the Daily Mail (February 9 2009) about a young boy who has bludgeoned his father to death after a prescription of Fluoxetine (Prozac). In young people in particular, Prozac is known to increase the risk of suicidal and aggressive tendencies. This is a major concern in young people as GPs continue to prescribe Prozac to young adults even with this knowledge.

I recently consulted with a young lady who had suffered mild-depression and was subsequently placed on Prozac. Within 10 days of starting the medication, she attempted suicide. She was lucky enough to have been found very quickly after taking an overdose of painkillers, and her life was saved. She came in to see me along with her mother, and both agreed that she had never suffered from suicidal tendencies prior to taking the Prozac. During her hospital stay, a diagnosis of Personality Disorder was made which stunned the family as the diagnosis did not fit with the person that they knew. The family felt that the Prozac had affected their daughter in very substantially damaging ways. She now wanted a better solution. Interestingly enough, this young woman's depression had started soon after the onset of an inflammatory bowel condition!

There is an ethical question when young individuals are treated with antidepressants. Despite numerous double-blind studies which indicate that antidepressants are no more effective than placebos in treating depression in children and adolescents, such medications continue to be widely prescribed. In an attempt to protect the lucrative market, companies such as GlaxoSmithKline have obscured suicide risks associated with profitable antidepressants for more than 15 years, as shown by court documents released recently. Only under duress and with a court order did GlaxoSmithKline alert people to raised suicide risks associated with the drugs Paroxetine and Seroxat.

The table below lists just some of the typical side-effects of anti-depressants:

Antidepressant type	Brand names	Documented side effects
Monoamine oxidase Inhibitors (MAOIs)	Nardil Parnate	Rapid, very high and dangerous increase in blood pressure if interactions with foods containing tyramine. Sleep disturbance, dry mouth, impotence, skin rash and blurred vision.
Tricyclics (TCAs)	Amitriptyline Clomipramine	Dry mouth, blurred vision, heart palpitations, constipation, sweating, sedation, weight gain, cardiovascular problems, impotence, reduced libido, mania. Fatal when taken as overdose.
Selective Serotonin reuptake inhibitors (SSRIs)	Fluoxetine (Prozac) Paroxetine (Paxil) Sertraline (Zoloft)	Increased anxiety, nausea, headaches, sexual dysfunction. Has fewer cardiac side-effects than TCAs. Increases suicide risk in youths.
Atypical	Effexor	Nausea, excessive sleeping, dry mouth, dizziness, constipation, nervousness.

For all of the reasons above, I very strongly believe that anti-depressants should be used as a last resort when all other contributing factors have been addressed or ruled out. It is important to work closely with your practitioner to correct the real reason underlying your anxiety or depression, instead of merely masking symptoms with an anti-depressant.

As for anxiety, medication should also not be the first course of action. Less than one third of individuals who are prescribed medications such as diazepam will find relief from anxiety. More often, the side effects such as weight gain, gastric upset, disturbed sleep will cause people to search for alternatives.

Coming off anti-depressants

Coming off anti-depressants can be really difficult, and withdrawal symptoms can be so severe that many people choose to remain on the medication. There are ways to reduce and stop your anti-depressants without experiencing these side-effects, but you must do this very gradually with the help and support of your doctor. Patients often ask how they would know when they were ready to come off their anti-depressants. I believe that because of the severity of the withdrawal symptoms, I always recommend working with a skilled practitioner so that you have a safety net in place.

Before you begin to reduce the anti-depressant, follow the 10 step plan at the back of this book. Firstly, make sure that you have your diet sorted out so that the right nutrition is going into the body to support the natural production of your neurotransmitters. You're going to need all the right nutrition to make sure your body can sustain the production of several required neurotransmitters.

Secondly, exercise is a proven way to lift the mood so make sure that you also have an exercise program firmly in place (not just on paper!). You should begin your exercise program at least 8 weeks before you plan to start coming off your medication. There are several herbal remedies that are helpful during the withdrawal (including Avena sativa) and those that can be used once you have stopped the anti-depressants (St John's wort). Once again, it is best to work with a qualified practitioner when using natural remedies.

If there are any underlying conditions such as a wheat allergy, thyroid or blood sugar imbalance make sure that these are addressed and stable before attempting to reduce the dosage. You should ask your GP or practitioner to rule all of possible underlying causes out first.

CHAPTER 5

What's the fix?

Some of you may have skipped right to this part, eager to find a quick fix. The conditions that have led to you to anxiety and depression, however, are most likely quite complex. To find the underlying causes will require some unravelling. For a successful outcome, it is important to understand why anxiety or depression may have started in the first place so that the patterns that trigger these conditions for you can be eliminated.

For instance, we have spoken in depth about how bowel or gut conditions affect mental health. Although anti-depression or anxiety medication or therapy will initially help, unless the underlying 'gut' problem is solved, these conditions will recur. It is therefore essential to understand what causes anxiety and/or depression in your particular case.

Breaking the cycle of these conditions require removing the causing or contributing factors that have caused your condition to develop in the first place to prevent re-occurrence. It is then essential that you replace them with more beneficial options that not only will prevent a re-occurrence of your condition, but that will strengthen the mind.

This will be a very individual process for each person, as the conditions leading up their anxiety or depression would have been unique. You may be able to clearly see what is causing your condition, or you may need to work with a skilled therapist to help pinpoint the causes.

Breaking the cycle

In the image below, one can see how underlying health problems, stress, poor nutrition, gut problems and environment can contribute to triggering the sympathetic nervous system. In the short term a heightened sympathetic nervous system helps the person respond very quickly to stress by increasing the heart rate, releasing adrenalin, inhibiting digestion and releasing glucose from the liver. All energy is shunted to the heart and muscles, thus mobilizing the body to fight or run (fight or flight). Once this powerful system is activated, the body is geared up to physically fight or escape. In our modern world, however, we cannot physically escape from our stress. We cannot run out of that meeting or hit the manager, although we'd sometimes like to! Instead, we are stuck in boardrooms or confined to cars, feeling stressed about that work meeting that we're late for, but having no physical outlet for stress. In the long run, this adversely affects our health by creating unbalanced blood sugar levels, stress on the cardiovascular system, disturbed sleep patterns and suffering mental health.

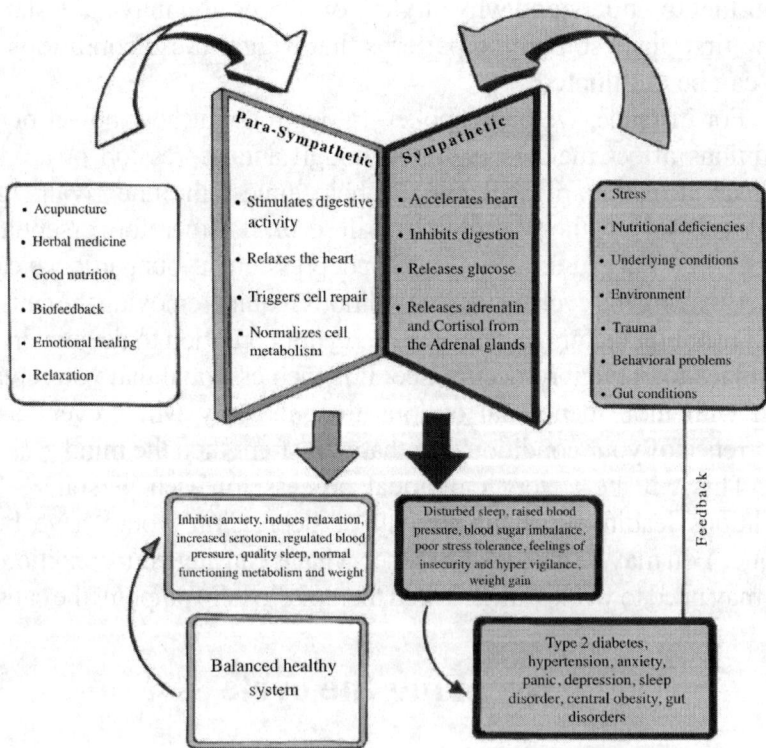

Image 6: The effects of the two branches of the nervous system

The sympathetic nervous system when triggered causes an alteration in the way in which the adrenal glands, which are two very small glands that sit above the kidneys, release adrenalin and cortisol. Adrenalin and cortisol, when secreted over a long period of time alter our physiology causing high blood pressure, sleep disorders, weight gain to name just a few. These conditions in turn, add to the stress that triggers the nervous system, thus keeping it in a feedback loop. For instance, trauma may have triggered the nervous system initially and if the situation continues for some time the result may be high blood pressure which in turn places more stress on the body.

As you can see, to break the pattern requires intervention. It requires a shift to the parasympathetic branch of the nervous system where body repair can take place. When in the parasympathetic state, the body and mind are in a state of balance and the person feels relaxed, calm and focused. Sometimes the shift to the parasympathetic state can happen naturally when the stressful trigger is removed, but at other times even when the stress is removed, the person remains anxious or depressed. It is then that a little extra help is needed from herbal remedies or therapies such as acupuncture, biofeedback, counselling etc.

The 10 step process in this book has been designed to help you work through, and eliminate all the factors that may be contributing to depression and anxiety for you. By following the 10 steps, you will be able to take control of your mental health, breaking the cycle of depression and anxiety:

The 10 steps to a healthy mind:

1. Clear out junk from the diet
2. Look at what you're putting in. Make sure you're getting enough healthy nutrients in the diet. Add variety to the diet including fresh fruits and vegetables, seeds and nuts. Balance blood sugar.
3. Treat underlying physical conditions, especially allergies, metabolic issues and any bowel conditions. Go to www.acuhealthuk.com and fill in the mental health questionnaire to help identify possible contributing factors for your condition.

4. Find time for meditation and relaxation. Everyone enjoys different things – some like walking in a park, others painting or formal meditation. Do what suits you, and don't force yourself into formal meditation if the mind is not able to settle.

5. Engage in emotional healing – read books that support this or use therapies such as Emotional Freedom Tecnique (EFT).

6. Make time for exercise, and even if you don't have the resources (time or money) to join a gym, take the stairs whenever you can, walk instead of taking the bus or driving. Qigong is the most effective exercise, in my opinion, for anxiety and depression.

7. Take responsibility for your own health!

8. Get enough sunshine; so make sure you get outside when the sun shines!

9. Get enough good sleep.

10. Get rid of energy drains.

In each of the sections I will discuss some of the ways in which the cycle of stress, anxiety and depression can be broken using the 10 steps.

10 Steps to achieving a healthy mind:

Step 1: Clear out junk

Most people that I see are not initially aware how important their diet is in inducing or in many cases eradicating their symptoms. However, people do want to have control over their own situations, and most are therefore very happy to make changes to the diet. Once they do, they are often amazed at the difference they experience.

One cannot think well, love well, sleep well,

if one has not dined well.

Virginia Woolf

Given how substantial even small biochemical changes in the brain may be, it's not surprising that a body of research is emerging which shows that artificial additives in our foods may be as powerful as drugs in contributing to panic, anxiety and depression. The first of the 10 steps described in this book for breaking the cycle of depression and anxiety involve clearing all the junk out of the diet. It may, as you will see, be one of the most important steps towards gaining a healthy mind.

I recently bumped into a patient of mine that I had previously treated for panic attacks. I was amazed to see someone I knew with severe agoraphobia in a bustling shopping centre. She was delighted to see me, and explained how during her first session of Resonance Biofeedback, we had identified that there was a possible overload of aspartame in the body. She had been in the habit of drinking a fizzy drink each day. She had avoided this additive for a few weeks, and made some other changes to her diet, and has never had a panic attack since!

This is an example of how a chemical which has been deemed safe by the European Food Safety Authority (EFSA) caused debilitating panic attacks for one individual. In fact, one of the first things I look at when patients are presenting with panic is aspartame consumption. In many cases, just making simple changes to the diet can resolve panic attacks.

The EFSA now recognizes that food colours and preservatives such as sodium benzoate can alter the behaviour of normal, healthy children. In practice I have seen this several times, and one instance was particularly remarkable. A young boy was in the waiting room while his sister was in for treatment with another practitioner. I had seen this young boy on several occasions, waiting quietly and patiently in the waiting room. This particular day, however, his grandmother was almost in tears of frustration as the boy had been impossible to manage. If you've ever been into a Jan de Vries clinic, you will also know that the clinics are all decorated with beautiful and priceless antiques, so no wonder grandma was a bit ruffled! The boy wasn't my patient, but I did stop to talk to the grandmother. She explained that her grandson was by nature always calm and quiet, and she had "no idea what had gotten into him". Aspartame was what had gotten into him! We quickly figured out that just minutes before his behaviour had changed, this boy had consumed a children's drink known to be very high in aspartame!

Making dietary changes does take some effort and discipline, and often the body tends to crave the "offenders"! However, these changes can often bring about lasting relief to those suffering from panic, terror, anxiety and even depression! Most importantly, read the labels. Always. If there are bits in there you don't understand, dump it! These are all artificial additives. You can begin right away on the 10 step plan by eliminating all the "junk" from your diet.

Foods to avoid

There are various foods/drinks that you should avoid which may be triggering depression or anxiety for you:

Alcohol:

The immediate effect of alcohol may be calming for most people. But as alcohol is metabolised by your body, it can cause anxiety-like symptoms. Women, who experience anxiety, mood swings, depression and PMS should avoid alcohol entirely or limit its use to occasional small amounts. Alcohol is rapidly absorbed by the body and like other sugars, alcohol increases hypoglycemia symptoms; excessive use can increase anxiety and mood swings.

Caffeine:

This stimulant can make you feel jittery and nervous and interfere with sleep. Coffee also reduces the body's magnesium levels which in itself can lead to anxiety. Caffeine is found in tea, coffee, cola, chocolate and some over the counter medications. One small study was carried out on patients whose depression was thought to be due to dietary factors. The researchers asked patients to cut out caffeine and sugar from the diet. Results showed that depressed people who cut out caffeine and sugar showed significantly more improvement than the control group. The same researchers later published an article in the Journal of Abnormal Psychology showing that reducing sugar intake in individuals helped to create emotional stability.

Withdrawing coffee/tea may initially cause a lot of discomfort including headaches and fatigue, but this will only last a few days and will be worth the effort. Recent research done by researchers at Durham University has also shown that caffeine consumers are more likely to suffer delusions. We know that caffeine stimulates large amounts of the stress hormone cortisol to be released which triggers a cascade of neurological changes within the body.

Aspartame:

Fizzy drinks not only contain large amounts of sugar, but they also very often contain aspartame which is a known trigger for anxiety, brain tumours and multiple sclerosis. This artificial sweetener which is abundant in food and drinks has now been linked to severe depression, irritability, aggression, anxiety, personality changes, insomnia, phobias, headaches, migraine, confusion, memory loss, dizziness, unsteadiness, numbness in the limbs, sleepiness, drowsiness, restless legs and tremors. As I've mentioned previously, I have seen personality changes happen quite quickly when even small amounts of aspartame have been consumed. In the same way, I have known several patients to resolve anxiety, insomnia and depression by simply avoiding this sweetener.

Aspartame, once in the body, breaks down into formaldehyde and has a particular liking for the cells of the nervous systems. Aspartame in the brain kills certain neurons by allowing the influx of too much calcium into the cells, which "excites" or stimulate the neural cells to death! There are several well documented studies now that link aspartame consumption not only with anxiety, but also brain tumors and cancer.

Processed foods:

Processed foods (canned, bottled or pre-packaged) are most often changed from their original state by heating, additives, preservatives, colourings, salt and sugar. Purchase only foods that are in their natural state. Processed foods are of course more convenient - that's what it comes down to. It's so much easier to pop something pre-prepared into the microwave! Convenience, however, isn't the only thing you get when you eat processed foods. There's a whole list of ingredients that manufacturers add, and we don't as yet know the long-term effects that they may have on the brain chemistry. Keep it simple. If you don't know what something is on label, don't eat it!

It is challenging when you lead a busy and chaotic life, and people often complain of having lack of time to prepare foods from scratch. If you cannot avoid processed foods, at least look at labels and try to find the most natural products without a long list of additives.

Refined foods:

Refined foods have gone through a process of bleaching, softening and fluffing – basically all the processes that makes the food have its unbelievable smooth or fluffy texture White bread, pastries, cakes have often undergone heavy processing. Once again, look at the labels and take care of what you eat. The flour used in most supermarket breads, pastries and cakes is so refined that it lacks vital nutrients like magnesium. Moreover, many of the chemicals used in the manufacturing of these products actually 'leach' good nutrients from the body.

Cold and uncooked foods:

In Traditional Chinese Medicine (TCM,) it is believed that the majority of the diet should be lightly cooked to 'predigest' the food. Although some nutrients are destroyed in cooking, the process of cooking renders nutrients much easier to absorb. In addition, cold foods themselves damage the Stomach & Spleen in TCM, which are closely related to depression and anxiety. This is especially important if you have any of the following symptoms: cold hands and feet, loose stools, undigested food in the stools, dizziness and aversion to cold.

Damp creating foods:

Interestingly in TCM, sugars, fat and dairy also damage the Spleen creating dampness which commonly contributes to depression. Ice cream, for instance, is one of the most damaging foods for the Spleen considering that it's a combination of sugar and dairy and it is cold! Wheat is also dampening and most people with depression do feel a difference when they eliminate dairy and wheat from their diets.

Sugar:

Excess sugar consumption can have a variety of consequences on the body. As we've seen, any disruption to either the gastrointestinal system or the metabolic system, can put us at greater risk for developing mental health conditions.

Firstly, sugar can disrupt the gastrointestinal tract by increasing the acidity leading to indigestion, malabsorption, increasing the risk of Crohn's disease and ulcerative colitis. Sugar also fuels the uncontrolled growth of Candida Albicans, a yeast infection which can disrupt gastrointestinal function. There is evidence that sugar disrupts the enzymatic processes that helps create neurotransmitters in the brain, can cause depression and affects learning.

Sugar should be avoided as much as possible for individuals prone to depression and anxiety and only very rarely consumed. Look for hidden forms of sugar in labels such as glucose, fructose, sucrose, corn syrup, molasses, honey, dextrose, lactose, maltose, galactose and concentrated grape juice. These are all concentrated forms of sugar and can detrimentally affect your blood sugar balance.

Step 1: Foods to Avoid Checklist

- Alcohol
- Caffeine containing drinks and foods such as coffee, tea and chocolate
- Aspartame
- Processed foods
- Refined foods
- Cold, raw foods
- Damp creating foods such as sugar, dairy and wheat
- Sugar, including glucose, lactose, corn syrup, sucrose etc.

Step 2: Replenish nutrients

"We must realize, however, that all living cells are continuously subject to imperfect nutrition and that overt mental disease is *known* to result from malnutrition, as, for example, in pellagra. In the light of these considerations, we would be foolhardy indeed to take for granted that the nutrition of the brain cells is automatically satisfactory in those who are afflicted or threatened with mild or severe mental disease."

Dr. Roger J, Williams, writing in *Nutrition Against Disease.*

Nutrient deficiencies and mental health

Nutritional deficiencies very often underlie mental health conditions and so getting the right nutrition is absolutely critical. The second step in our plan to creating a healthy mind involves making sure that our nutritional status is optimal, ensuring that the right mix of ingredients is available to build a healthy mind.

Magnesium deficiency:

If you suffer from anxiety coupled with heart palpitations, irritability, depression, twitching, trembling, insomnia, fibromyalgia, muscle cramps or any connective tissue disease, there may be a magnesium deficiency. Magnesium is needed to relax muscles, and is biochemically needed to turn off the release of adrenalin! A very large study involving more than 5000 individuals found a correlation between magnesium dietary intake, and lower levels of both anxiety and depression.

Most people do not get the required amounts of magnesium that the body and mind needs to function optimally, and so anxiety and depression creeps in. Food sources of magnesium include buckwheat, parsley, spinach, almonds, cashews, oats and halibut. A magnesium supplement may be required if you do not get enough magnesium from the diet, but dietary sources are always superior.

Several other studies show a link between mental health and magnesium levels, including studies involving schizophrenia, anxiety and depression. In one study, researchers fed mice a diet deficient in magnesium and then watched their behaviour. The group of mice fed on the low magnesium diet showed significantly higher levels of depression and anxiety than mice fed a balanced diet.

As magnesium can sometimes make the stools looser, transdermal magnesium which absorbs through the skin is a much better option for those with gut issues.

Tryptophan deficiency and serotonin

Tryptophan is an amino acid that is not produced by the body but comes strictly from the diet. It is particularly plentiful in chocolate (hooray! but make sure it is 70% dark chocolate), oats, bananas, dried dates, cottage cheese, meat, fish, turkey and peanuts.

In the brain, tryptophan converts to serotonin, the neurotransmitter responsible for feelings of well-being, calmness, relaxation, confidence and concentration. When serotonin levels decrease, depression sets in. The only source for serotonin in the brain is tryptophan. So, if there is not enough tryptophan in the diet, serotonin (and subsequently melatonin) is not produced which results in anxiety, depression and sleep disturbance. This is what is known as the Serotonin Deficiency Syndrome.

There is clinical research that confirms tryptophan's effectiveness as a natural sleeping aid. In people who are anxious, agitated and depressed tryptophan can restore well-being and behavioural self-control. Research has shown that in people suffering from depression, combining the amino acid tyrosine with tryptophan works better than just tryptophan on its own.

Supplemental tryptophan has also been used to reduce anger and aggression. A deficiency of tryptophan can cause symptoms ranging from depression, PMS, anxiety, alcoholism, insomnia, violence, aggression, suicidal tendencies, memory decline and compulsive behaviour.

vitamin B12 deficiency

A literature search of vitamin B12 deficiency will bring up a range of studies and papers on mental health. The most common symptoms noted in vitamin B12 deficiency are depression, mania, psychotic symptoms, cognitive impairment and obsessive compulsive behaviour. Other symptoms include menstrual problems, a sore tongue and low resistance to infection.

Vitamin B12 is an essential vitamin for brain and heart function and certain individuals (although we don't fully understand why) appear to need higher quantities of vitamin B12. This must not be confused with the condition called pernicious anemia which often occurs in the elderly. In this case patients are unable to absorb vitamin B12, leading to a severe shortage of the vitamin which results in irreversible brain damage.

What we are talking about here is a milder deficiency, which is easily missed. Although the vitamin levels may only be marginally reduced, the depression is anything but mild. Usually there is a feeling of listlessness as well as unclear or "foggy" thinking. It is thought that in patients presenting with depression, a vitamin B12 deficiency contributes in about 30% of cases. Vitamin B12 has also been linked to disturbed sleep-wake cycles where the person tends to fall asleep only very late at night and then has difficulty waking in the morning.

Making changes

Coping with anxiety disorder and/or depression can be difficult. But there are several things you can do on your own to reduce your anxiety and to lift your mood. One of the most important things you can do is to get the right nutrition. This means eating a balanced diet, taking nutritional supplements if appropriate, and limiting or avoiding foods that may cause or mimic anxiety and depression.

In the section "Brain Matters- is it all in my mind?" the neurotransmitters are outlined with a description of their functions as well as the nutrients that are required to synthesize their building blocks. Without the right ingredients, the body is unable to synthesise the neurotransmitters that keep the mind and emotions in balance.

I have seen many patients who have 'cured' themselves from anxiety and depression by making significant changes to their diets, and you can too by keeping to a few nutritional principles.

- Increase your intake of complex carbohydrates. Carbohydrate-rich meals and snacks are thought to increase the amount of serotonin in your brain, which has a calming effect. This includes brown rice, oats, oatcakes, rice cakes etc.

- **Eat frequent small meals during the day.**

  Going too long between meals can result in low blood sugar, which can cause nervousness and irritability. Also, eat more complex carbohydrates (starches mentioned above) and fewer simple carbohydrates (sugars). Complex carbohydrates take longer to break down, which helps prevent a sudden drop in blood sugar.

- **Stay well-hydrated**

  Even mild dehydration can affect your mood, increasing anxiety.

- **Drink more green tea!**

  Research on human volunteers has demonstrated that L-theanine, a compound found abundantly in green tea, creates a sense of relaxation approximately 30-40 minutes after ingestion. L-theanine directly stimulates the production of alpha brain waves, creating a state of deep relaxation and mental alertness similar to what is achieved through meditation.

- **Mood foods**

  Eat more of the following foods (unless you have a specific allergy or intolerance to any of these foods): yoghurt, fresh fruit, vegetables, wholegrain (oats, rice), turkey, chicken, eggs, fish, baked potato etc. Complex carbohydrates (wholegrain bread and pasta) can act as mild tranquilisers by increasing the amount of serotonin in your brain. Avocado, banana, red plum, tomatoes, pineapples, eggplants and walnuts all contain the precursor amino acids for producing serotonin

  Enjoy foods that contain tryptophan, an amino acid that your body converts to serotonin. This includes bananas, oats, soy, poultry, nuts, peanut butter and sesame seeds.

Nutritional testing is possible to determine any specific deficiencies that there may be (see appendix). In most cases, testing will not be necessary after a healthy, varied diet is implemented. In some cases, however, deficiencies may be deep seated and will require temporary supplementation.

The rule in step two is to keep the diet as natural as possible and full of variety.

Step 3: Resolve underlying physical conditions

If you have taken the first steps in rectifying the diet and you do not notice a considerable improvement it is necessary to investigate underlying conditions that may be contributing to low moods or anxiety. Start by taking the online questionnaire www.acuhealthuk.com which will help highlight possible areas of concern. If an underlying condition is detected, make sure it gets treated as priority.

Step 4: Meditation & Relaxation

Both depression and anxiety respond very well to a natural approach, but I have found that without learning how to relax both the mind and body, the natural medicines do not work as well. Among the easiest methods to quiet the body and mind are relaxation exercises. Some of the popular techniques are meditation, prayer, progressive relaxation and self-hypnosis. The type of relaxation technique best for each person is totally individual, and you may have to do a little experimenting to find out what works best for you. Meditation can be a powerful way to learn to relax and control the mind, but it's not for everyone. If you are not able to calm the mind in the first place, you may be creating unrealistic expectations when it comes to meditation and the result may just be frustration. Do what you know will relax you, whether it's a walk in nature or listening to relaxing music, but pay attention to the way that you feel during your relaxation time – become aware of your emotional radar.

The important thing is to set aside at least 15 to 20 minutes each day for your relaxation practice. There are also many different types of relaxation tapes on the market. Find one that you enjoy and relax with. I'll never forget one frustrated patient who told me that he continued listening to a relaxation audio tape for weeks on end, even though the voice on the tape unnerved and annoyed him. At the end of listening to the tape he was completely wound up. Eventually he changed the tape to a voice that he found more soothing, and was finally able to relax. This reminds me that we're so individual and what works for the goose may not necessarily work for the gander!

Step 5: Heal emotional scars

Old emotional scars can lie under the surface of our current emotions. My good friend, and colleague, Moira calls it the reference library. Many of our current emotions and behaviours are in response to previous experiences we have had. The nervous system is adaptable to the environment in which it finds itself, but as we travel through life, we build up a reference library and often our emotional responses are triggered by something in the past. For instance, for someone who has had an unfaithful partner in the past, mistrust sometimes carries over into new relationships, causing emotional difficulties. Clearing out the emotional reference library can be very liberating for the mind and soul. There are many aspects involved in emotional healing including most importantly, forgiveness. There are many helpful therapies such as acupuncture, counselling, Emotional Freedom Technique and homeopathy which can be very helpful in emotional healing.

Step 6: Exercise

There are numerous studies that show a strong positive effect of exercise in particular for depression, but also anxiety to an extent. It is not a magic bullet but research shows that as little as 30 minutes of exercise per day can significantly reduce the effects of both depression and anxiety. It isn't quite understood how it works, but one theory is that exercise releases endorphins which help to make us feel good. Regular exercise is also known to regulate sleep patterns. When depression has made you feel low and exhausted, starting an exercise program can be challenging. However, the benefits are huge and well worth the effort!

Aerobic exercise appears to have the strongest positive effect on depression. This means doing physical activity that raises the heartbeat at least 80% above the normal resting rate and keeps it there for 20 minutes or more. To calculate this, measure your pulse rate by placing your fingers on the pulsing artery on the front side of your neck. Time how many beats you have per minute. Multiply your resting heart rate by 0.8. Now add this value to your resting heart rate to get your aerobic threshold. During exercise, you can measure your pulse at 5 minute intervals – aiming to get to the aerobic threshold.

Exercise should be done at least 3 times a week for the cumulative effect to become noticeable. If you haven't been exercising for a while, start small. Walk instead of taking the bus, or take stairs instead of the elevator. Even small starts can boost your morale. It is important to find exercise that you enjoy and that you will be able to stick to, so you might need to experiment to find something that suits you.

Often people complain of not having time to exercise. I believe that the benefits we receive from exercising reach so far into our lives that we tend to get more done. I certainly know that the times that I have exercised, I seemed to have more energy and strangely enough, more time to accomplish what I wanted to do.

Step 7: Take responsibility for your own health

One of the most essential keys to healing, in my opinion, is being able to take responsibility for your own health. This means not blaming others for your state of health. Now that we've discussed emotions leading to disease, it is easy to blame others for your ill-health. Your spouse may not behave the way that you would like him to, or a relative may continuously vex you leading to anger, frustration or sadness. However, we all have a choice about how we deal with these emotions, and recognizing them and working with them, will create a healthier and happier person rather than brooding about them.

How to take responsibility

Taking responsibility also includes not blaming others (partners, parents, genes, doctors or health care professionals) for your condition, or expecting a doctor or therapist to 'make you better'. When you shift responsibility for your health onto others, you take the healing power away from yourself.

Remember, health care professionals can only guide you and make recommendations, but ultimately you are the one who needs to manage your own health and well-being. Good healthcare practitioners will gently lead you to know and challenge yourself. You are solely responsible for what you put into your mouth, what comes out of your mouth in spoken word, how you deal with your emotions, how you treat your body, which therapies you undertake to facilitate healing, the mindset that you allow yourself to enjoy, etc... Nobody will care as much about your own well-being as your own self, and you have a vested interest in seeing your health improve!

I only truly began my own recovery when I took responsibility for my own health. I also remember consulting with a woman once who came in pleading for me to "make her better". "I'm afraid I can't do that" I said. "What I can do is help you and direct you to be able to do it for yourself". We worked together for a little while, and slowly she began to take more responsibility for herself and her recovery has been truly remarkable. In fact, she now gets actively every aspect of her treatment plan!

To be honest, there are many times when people are not willing to take responsibility for their own health, and then there is not much that I or anyone else (or a prescription) can do. Often when people do not respond to any form of treatment, there is usually something they have to discover for themselves.

Step 8: Bathe in natural sunlight

Sunlight is a natural anti-depressant and we all feel better on sunny days. The reason for this section, however, is that I am writing this book in Edinburgh where many of my patients will be sunlight deficient because of the climate.

Mood, as we have seen is influenced by many complex inter-related factors. Several studies have shown low levels of vitamin D (the vitamin made by the body during sun exposure) is linked to depression although scientists can not confirm whether low vitamin D levels lead to depression, or whether depression causes low vitamin D levels.

Serotonin levels are known to increase with exposure to bright light and most people will agree that their moods are elevated in the summer months. As the body stores vitamin D, doctors also think that sunlight exposure in the summer could impact how you feel months down the line.

Light stimulates the production of a compound called cholecalciferol, which the body eventually transforms into vitamin D. The more sun exposure you get during summer, the higher the stores of vitamin D will be over the dark winter months.

I would recommend spending at least 30 minutes a day outdoors, early morning and late afternoon being the best times to avoid high radiation. Spend coffee breaks and lunch breaks outside to increase your daily exposure.

If you know that you are not getting sufficient vitamin D, a supplement may be required.

Step 9: Get enough good sleep

There are often sleep issues linked to depression and anxiety and it was traditionally believed that depression and anxiety cause sleep disturbance. However, researchers at the Western Australian Centre for Health and Ageing believe that lack of sleep could lead to depression. The researchers there are concerned that the use of sleeping tablets that are so often prescribed for depression may actually exacerbate depression.

Most books will list sleeping problems as a symptom of depression and anxiety, which certainly it is, but very importantly; a poor sleep pattern can also result in these conditions.

One reason that sleep is so very important is that most of the body's repair and restorative processes happen during this time. In fact, practitioners of TCM will always tell you that you should be in bed by 10pm, even if you are not sleepy, so that the repair to vital organs can begin.

To promote better sleep, one should keep a regular bedtime routine. Steer clear of sleeping pills even though they may give you short-term relief – in the long run they can disrupt sleep patterns further.

Pay attention to pre-bedtime diet. Avoid stimulants such as tea, coffee, chocolate and soft drinks after 2pm. If your bladder is waking you at night, minimise liquid from the early evening. Regular exercise is known to improve sleep quality. Make sure that the bedroom is dark with no street or electronic light present. Lastly, keep a regular bedtime. Even if you are not tired, keep to a regular and consistent bed time.

Step 10: Get rid of energy drains

Energy drains are activities or people that leave you feeling depleted in energy, anxious or low in mood. These are very individual things, so you will need to make a list of things that energize you and those that leave you feeling low or depleted. For instance, procrastination, perfectionism and worry are common drains. Striving for perfection can be exhausting. Putting things off (procrastinating) mean that issues are always at the back of your mind. Worry can be a huge energy drain. Begin to notice your individual draining patterns. Once you are aware of them it becomes easier to change them.

Things such as nature, recreation, or massage, however, can leave us feeling replenished and refreshed. Once you've made the list, try and find ways in which you can reduce the amount of time or energy you spend on the items in the "energy drains" side, and see if you can increase the amount of time you spend doing things that replenish you. Below, I will discuss some of the more common energy drains, but what drains one person may energize another. For instance, I work day in and day out with people affected by anxiety, depression, cancer and ill health. Although my work is challenging and emotionally demanding, I am energized by my work because I get my adrenalin buzz from seeing patients progress! My husband, however, is an introvert and finds working with people stressful and draining on his energy resources. So, this part of the process will be entirely individual to you.

Negative people

Have you ever noticed that spending time with some people leave you feeling drained, exhausted and depressed? Some people can be "energy vampires", and in some cases this can be very noticeable, in others; more subtle. Even though they may not overtly be demanding energy from you, they may be doing so by involving you in their dramas, or always complaining, or by trying to gain your approval by being overly nice. In most cases, energy drainers are those who do not take care of their own emotional needs, and so rely on external validation, love and affection from others to the point of draining them. Are there people in your life who talk incessantly about themselves or who involve you in their life dramas? They may be subtly (or sometimes not so subtly) making your depression worse. When you are suffering from depression, it is important that you protect yourself from negative people and situations.

Many of us allow energy drains to continue because we don't want to hurt the other person's feelings, so we keep quiet or avoid the person. For instance, you may get drawn into situations that you resent or you may not say the things that are important. In doing so, it means that you are not taking care of yourself, or honouring your own needs, which opens you up to depression.

When you don't speak up about how you really feel, you are not taking responsibility for your own feelings and putting the other person's feelings or needs ahead of your own. Now at this point, people often stop me and say that it sounds very selfish to put your own needs ahead of others. At first it may appear so, but you will quickly begin to see that you can never be responsible for others' feelings or needs; only your own. If you don't take care of your own feelings, you will begin to resent yourself for being drawn into situations you don't want to be in. I once had a patient who continued to go on several dates with a man she never liked just because she did not want to hurt his feelings. In the end, she began to resent this man and it all bottled up until she exploded one night and he couldn't understand what had happened.

It happens so often that it is difficult to set boundaries with people who drain you. You may end up unwillingly spending time with the energy drainer, and resent that person for the time you are giving them. In the end, the time and energy that you give the person is not given freely with genuine love, but with resentment. This is a toxic and very unhealthy situation. When we give of our time and energy, it should be done freely and with love.

One patient, Sheila, was spending hours a week on the phone to her sister, and feeling very drained after each call, she was starting to avoid her sister to conserve her energy but the feelings of guilt was eating away at her. She would come into her sessions feeling guilty about avoiding her sister's calls, lest she gets drawn into a 2 hour conversation. We worked out some strategies to deal with the situation and she spoke openly to her sister about how she was feeling. Although her sister was initially hurt, they were able to work out specific times when they would speak, and kept those conversations limited to 15 minutes. She felt the resentment for the draining phone calls beginning to diminish, and was then able to talk to her sister with much more love, compassion and care.

When I saw Sheila a few months later, she was a different person. Now with new boundaries in place, her relationship with her sister had greatly improved and she even looked forward to a visit from her sister, which in the past would have been an event she dreaded.

I must also add that there will be times when family or good friends, who have always been energy-givers, are experiencing difficult times and require emotional support. In order for you to be able to support your friend or family member, you have to be clear about how much support you can offer given your current situation, and then do so fully with love and compassion. In other words, openly saying to someone, I want to be there for you and I have capacity to give you an hour during which time I am going to give you 100% of my attention.

I see patients every day for hours on end, and so I also have to be clear about the boundaries of support that I can offer. I can listen and offer advice when I am in the clinic. I can do so with a sense of love and true compassion. I cannot, however, spend hours on the phone in the evenings to all my patients who need support, as I have my own family. This does not mean that I don't love my job, and that I don't want to help others. When I first started practicing I felt that as a compassionate therapist I should be available at all times. Many times my husband and daughter would sit at the dinner table waiting and then eventually just take themselves off to bed as I was talking to patients on the phone. However, I would end up feeling that I had let my family down by putting others' needs ahead of theirs and felt tremendously sad about it. Nobody gained. I have since developed strict boundaries around family time. At first, it may seem hard to not make yourself available but in the long run it translates into stronger, healthier relationships.

How can you deal with energy draining people? You cannot stop the energy drain until you fully accept that you are not responsible for the other person's feelings. It is only when you feel that responsibility to the other person's feelings, that you get drained.

Once you can understand this concept and accept it, you can gently and with compassion remove yourself from situations that drain you. When you are taking responsibility for your own feelings, it is not difficult to end a phone conversation or walk away. One thing that usually helps is being clear at the outset about how much time you have and then ending a conversation is much easier. For instance, when your energy drainer phones you can say "I'm glad to hear from you. However, I've only got 5 minutes" at the outset. That way you can end the conversation without hurt.

Although this may seem difficult to do at first, you will begin to feel more positive about the way in which you manage relationships and overall feelings of positivity will grow.

Too many commitments

Many people will withdraw when depressed or anxious, depending on your nature, you may do the opposite and maintain a very busy schedule. Having a busy schedule may help you avoid facing up to the depression or anxiety, but will not serve you in the long run, as these conditions lurk in the background, waiting for a little break in your schedule. Sometimes doing too much also drains your energy and can stop you from dealing with the depression. Make a list of all your commitments, including work, family, voluntary, personal, etc. Now choose the ones that drain your energy without giving you much joy. Once you have identified the ones that are not giving you pleasure – give them up. It may seem impossible to do so, but saying 'no' can relinquish some of the energy drain. This will help protect your sanity, and free you up to do the things that give you joy.

Unfinished tasks

A long list of things that need doing means that our energy is tied up in worry, and this can really weigh heavily on your mind. Make a list of the things that you need to do, prioritise those that are urgent or bear the heaviest weight on your mind, and set aside time to do a few of those on the list each day. If a specific task seems too huge or overwhelming, break it up into smaller tasks and tackle it that way.

As you move through the list the burden will lighten, even if starting the task may initially feel overwhelming.

Unclean house

An unclean or untidy house can increase feelings of inadequacy, anxiety and or depression. If you are depressed, the mere thought of housework may have you feeling down. However, it is known that once we begin to clean up, clear clutter and organize the home, we begin to feel better. Having a home that is organized and aesthetic does lift the mood. Start by dedicating one day to cleaning your home inside out, and then maintain it daily by clearing mess as it happens. By not delaying any housework, it is easier to stay "on top" of getting it done by doing little bits daily. Also, find ways to enjoy the cleaning process. It shouldn't be an arduous task. Liven your cleaning up by playing your favorite uplifting music.

Television

Television can be not only a huge time-drainer, but also an energy drainer. Select your programs carefully, and watch only those that you are truly interested in and that uplift you. If you are flipping through channels, chances are you are watching out of boredom. Only put the television on for specific programs.

Relinquish control

Learning to let go of the issues that we don't have control over can free us from feelings of guilt, anger and responsibility. Trying to control situations or others (co-workers, kids, spouse, etc) can be very exhausting. Let it go! In doing so, you will experience less frustration, anger and resentment.

You may find it takes a bit of time and observation before you determine what your energy providers and energy drains are. The best way to gain an understanding is to constantly monitor how you are feeling in different situations. Very quickly, you will begin to see the patterns of energy providers and energy drains.

CHAPTER 6

Helpful Therapies

Resonance Biofeedback

The new field of energetic medicine has seen the creation of new sophisticated and intelligent technology based on quantum physics principles which can rapidly change the body's energy field to help ease depression.

According to the principles of energetic medicine, the body's mental well-being depends on information fields on the energetic or quantum field level. Using Resonance Biofeedback, we can detect disturbed informational fields which produce mental or emotional lows or dysfunctional patterns such as anxiety and/or depression. The correction of this imbalance can be accomplished by fixing these disturbances, which can then restore mental and emotional well being. Energetic medicine, by rebalancing the body and mind, enables the body and mind to heal itself, naturally.

Firstly in a Resonance Biofeedback (RB) session, the reactivity to specific neurotransmitters in the brain is tested to determine any imbalances. Keep in mind however, that these are not quantitative measurements, but are the body's reactivity to specific neurotransmitters. It is not at this stage possible to directly measure neurotransmitter levels without an invasive procedure. With RB we simply measure subconscious reactivity to a panel of neurotransmitters.

Once any imbalances are determined, we then energetically balance the high and the low neurotransmitters, boosting those that are in low supply. This can help to start lifting the depression fog and to calm anxiety. We also look at the connectivity between left brain and right brain which can create very severe depression and anxiety symptoms if not addressed. In the brain, there is a cord-like structure called the Corpus Callosum which helps the left and right brain communicate with one another. Several studies have shown that individuals with a weakened cord are prone to suffering from depression in particular. Harmonic therapy works by encouraging the brain to strengthen the connections between the left and right hemispheres. By stimulating the Corpus Callosum we encourage hemispheric communication of thoughts, information, and make neurotransmitter responses more effortless, efficient and profound.

Nervous system functioning is tested to determine whether the person is in a sympathetic or parasympathetic nervous state. Two major conditions are often picked up during the nervous system session. The first being a Sympathetic Imbalance or a Sympathetic Oscillation Disorder. Simply put, this means that the nervous system switches too easily to the fight and flight, even in situations where there is no actual threat, but often rather a perceived threat. The second imbalance that often shows up is a Vagus Nerve imbalance which can cause symptoms of anxiety mainly in the chest (tightness, palpitations) or gut (butterflies or diarrhea). If an imbalance is picked up, the nervous system is retrained using resonance pulses to behave in a more appropriate way.

Other factors we must then take into consideration include underlying causes of anxiety or depression such as hypoglycemia, thyroid disease and gut health.

The Resonance Biofeedback system has very powerful safety mechanisms which ensure that treatment is gentle and non-invasive.

Acupuncture

Acupuncture must be one of the most effective ways to naturally treat depression and anxiety without putting any chemicals into the body, and the only side effects are relaxation and improved health! Chinese physicians have been aware of the link between the gut and the brain for thousands of years. I remember reading in my acupuncture training that the mind is "created" from the functioning of the bowels and gut, and affected by external stimuli. At the time, I didn't realise just how valid that connection really is. Chinese Medicine believes that the mind arises as a function of the digestive organs and bowels, but the functioning of these organs is also affected by the experiences of the mind and emotions. These are in fact inseparable as Chinese medicine makes no dichotomy or division between the psychological and the physiological.

There have been several studies conducted on acupuncture and depression. One study, carried out at the University of Arizona in 1998 found acupuncture to be very effective in treating depression. At least 70% of the subjects in the study experienced at least 50% reduction of symptoms. Another National Institutes of Health (NIH) study showed that acupuncture is as effective as pharmacotherapy or psychotherapy as a treatment for depression. This is of particular importance to clinically depressed women who are pregnant and reluctant to use anti-depressant medication that could affect the development of their babies. On the other hand, the chronic stress of depression can itself be detrimental for mother and infant. Therefore, acupuncture is often recommended as a safe therapy during pregnancy.

In China, acupuncture treatments would be given every second day for several weeks. In the West, the cost of treatment does not make this intensive strategy as viable, but most patients respond very well treated twice a week for the first few weeks, and then gradually spacing the treatment further apart, until once a month is achieved as maintenance therapy. Maintenance treatments are recommended because depression does tend to recur.

Because acupuncturists treat the individual, they are less concerned with treatment protocols for depression or anxiety, or the western diagnosis or label you may have been given. Chinese medicine and acupuncture does not treat "depression" or "anxiety"; instead they treat the individual's disharmony or disease pattern, and do so with great success. Very often in the West, we like to label disease patterns (diabetes, migraine, etc.), and then researchers try to find a treatment cure for the disease. When they do, they often find that the treatment works in a percentage of the patients, but not in others. What they have missed sight of is the individual, and this is the one thing that Chinese medicine (and acupuncture) never, ever does. Your acupuncturist will not treat your depression only. They will treat you individually in a custom way considering each symptom and sign, and incorporating that into the treatment for a completely tailored treatment. In my experience, it is this approach that makes the treatment so highly successful. Keep in mind that not everyone practicing acupuncture are acupuncturists. Often physiotherapists and doctors will learn a short course on acupuncture (sometimes as little as 40 hours), and can apply limited acupuncture but without the understanding of the theory or principles that makes acupuncture powerful. Check the qualifications of the acupuncturist before you start treatment. Make sure that your practitioner is registered with an accrediting body such as the British Acupuncture Council to ensure that they have undergone rigorous training.

Homeopathy

I have had the privilege to work for many years alongside Jenny Livingstone, a very dedicated and skilled homeopath. Jenny and I have worked together on many of my more difficult cases and I have seen very good results with homeopathy. Jenny's training encompassed the traditional classical homeopathy but she has also ventured into studying and prescribing some of the more contemporary remedies with great success. So, when writing this book, I felt Jenny would be the perfect one to write a piece on homeopathy.

Jenny Livingstone writes:

In my experience as a Homeopath I have found homeopathy to be very helpful in treating stress, anxiety and depression. In fact very often some forms of mental and emotional stress can be at the bottom of other physical symptoms. In these cases homeopathy is most helpful because we aim to treat the roots of all symptoms and not just the bodily manifestation. This is what it means to take a holistic approach to health.

Many eczema sufferers will say that they notice their skin can flare up when they experience stress. One friend of mine developed eczema on his neck shortly after being made redundant from his job. The eczema would flare up every time he went for a job interview. I didn't give him a remedy for eczema; I gave him a remedy called Lycopodium. This remedy is primarily for lack of confidence combined with anxiety. Within weeks his entire skin problem had disappeared. This is an example of how Homeopaths will look for and then treat the roots of a problem and not just the surface. I have even seen chronic life long eczema disappear gradually with this approach.

It is a good idea to seek homeopathic treatment when you are undergoing a major life stress e.g. redundancy, bereavement, divorce and other traumas. The Homeopath would treat the stress and anxiety at the time and this can often prevent other illnesses from developing. Carefully chosen remedies can give you extra energy to move on through these life events and help you to grow from the experience.

The world is a rapidly changing place and I find that more and more people are coming to see me who have developed anxiety and depression as a result of the changes that have overwhelmed them. Constant stress erodes our life force and as we lose energy we might turn in on ourselves and become depressed. Homeopathic treatment can often prevent the onset of depression or it can help to lift you out of it and could prevent having to resort to antidepressant drugs. Very often homeopathic treatment raises people's energy so that they are able to make decisions and set their life back on a new and happier track.

Another part of the body which can be a target for stress related disorders is the gut. In fact the skin conditions which we notice coming from stress probably have their origin in the digestive system as the two are so closely connected. We easily see how fear can bring on diarrhoea. When nervous we talk about "butterflies in our tummy". Grief can shut down the appetite or provoke "comfort" eating. Over eating at night can cause insomnia. Even the medical profession agree that stomach ulcers and irritable bowel syndrome can be linked to stress.

In order to tackle the roots of these deep seated conditions it is best to consult a qualified Homeopath. However there are some self help methods of treating yourself which are really worth trying. You can go into many chemists and health stores and buy homeopathic remedies over the counter. They come in different potencies. The potency represents the strength of the remedy. In shops you usually get 6c or 30c and I recommend 30c, the higher potency, for most anxiety related conditions.

As a general rule you only need one tablet per dose. You only take the remedy while you have the symptoms. When the symptoms are strong you can repeat the dose every half an hour for three doses, then once an hour for three doses, then once every two hours if required for the rest of the day.

If the remedy is not helping the symptoms after several hours then it may be the wrong remedy or you may need a stronger potency. If the remedy is helping you, then only repeat the dose when symptoms return. Learn to follow your own body and mind and know what you need. Do not keep taking remedies when your symptoms have gone unless advised by a Homeopath.

Here are some remedies which you can easily buy to help you with stress and anxiety. The number one remedy for all fear and anxiety is **Aconite 30c**. It is also good to try if anxiety stops you from sleeping.

Arg. Nit. 30c is good for anticipatory nerves before a stressful event. This remedy can help with the diarrhoea which nerves can cause.

Nux.Vom. 30c is a powerful remedy for the digestive system and stress. This is more for people who respond to stress with anger rather than anxiety but they may not have an outlet for this anger. It is good to try **Nux.Vom** for stomach pain following stressful incidents. It is also good for people who wake up at 4a.m. thinking about work. Incidentally it is a very good hangover remedy as it detoxifies the liver.

I would like to recommend **Ignatia 30c** as a self help remedy for emotional upset. This is a remedy primarily for grief but it can be used for less intense emotions related to stress. Use it for tears, frustration, distress, and sadness. It is very calming and healing for these emotions. Remember that any situation of loss, including redundancy and divorce can also provoke feelings of grief. Even moving house to a new town can feel like a loss and **Ignatia** can often transform these feelings.

Try **Coffea 30c** made from the coffee bean to help you with insomnia. Aconite is for anxiety but if you are wide awake and over stimulated then **Coffea** is the remedy to try.

I carry many of these remedies around with me and use them regularly in daily life. They give me personally a great deal of benefit and it is my wish that more people will be able to access this. They are completely non toxic and are safe for babies and children and during pregnancy. As they are so highly diluted the homeopathic remedies can be taken alongside orthodox medication without harmful side effects. I hope you will include Homeopathy in your stress relief programme and that you would see the benefits that I see for my patients.

Phytotherapy

Herbs have been used for hundreds and sometimes thousands of years to treat depression and anxiety safely. There is solid evidence that herbal remedies do work very well for both anxiety and depression. It is important to be aware that natural remedies may often take longer to reach their effectiveness, but once they do there is often no difference between the effectiveness of the natural remedy and that of the synthetic drug, except fewer side effects!

Just a few of the remedies are discussed below but I would recommend seeing a qualified herbalist to make sure you get the right remedy for you.

Avena sativa

Avena sativa must be one of my favourite remedies. It is a very gentle, yet powerful nerve tonic that works to return a calm balance to the nervous system. With the appropriate dietary changes, Avena sativa can work wonders when there is nervous and mental exhaustion as well as anxiety. Research carried out by Edinburgh physicians showed that those using Avena sativa had quieter sleep (as measured by electroencephalogram (EEG)). It is also a good remedy to use to curb cravings, and is recommended for symptoms of withdrawal from nicotine and alcohol. It's a very safe remedy, and has no restrictions on its use other than in pregnancy and nursing.

Hypericum (St John's wort)

St John's wort is one of the most thoroughly researched natural remedies. Several studies have shown that Hypericum alleviates mild depression after about four weeks of treatment, without the side effects of conventional antidepressants. It is also a remedy often prescribed to patients affected by Seasonal Affective Disorder (SAD). It can be a very powerful remedy for those suffering from depression, and has the added benefits of increasing alertness and improving sleep. St John's wort, however, cannot be taken together with anti-depressants. It is essential to speak to your pharmacist or Doctor before taking this remedy, if you are on any prescription medications, as St John's wort can interfere with certain medications. While scientists are still unsure as to how it works, numerous studies have shown improvements in tiredness, mood, emotional fear and disturbed sleep.

Passiflora

Passiflora is a very frequently prescribed remedy when there is both anxiety and depression. It is often prescribed in menopause when anxiety and sleep disturbances arise. Like Avena sativa, it works on relaxing the nervous system, and positively affects both the physical and mental symptoms of stress. It has no restrictions on long-term use, but once again cannot be taken alongside other antidepressants or tranquilisers.

Valerian

Valerian is a natural sedative prescribed during times of stress, especially if there is a sleep disturbance. It is as effective as many conventional tranquilisers at calming the nervous system without the side effects associated with conventional tranquilisers (including addiction).

Black cohosh

Black cohosh has been recognized to correct mild depression and fatigue in both menopause and also in some women experiencing Premenstrual Syndrome (PMS). Black cohosh appears to work both directly on the hormones as well as the nervous system, and is often recommended to help not only with the physical changes of menopause, but also the emotional. Black cohosh cannot be taken alongside oral contraceptives, HRT or any other hormonal preparations such as Tamoxifen. Black cohosh can also not be tolerated by individuals with aspirin allergy.

Supplements

People often ask whether they should be taking supplements. As we've seen in the previous sections, nutrient deficiencies can cause severe depressive and anxious thinking. Although I still believe that it is critical to get nutrients from a balanced diet, it may sometimes be necessary to top-up with a supplement.

There are several books which address the issue of dietary deficiencies and mental health, one of the most comprehensive being Patrick Holford's Optimum Nutrition for the Mind. In his book, Holford emphasizes how individual these deficiencies may be. Nutritional testing can save money in the long run by ensuring that only the necessary supplements are given. Hair mineral analysis is one of determining your nutritional status, enabling a tailored nutritional programme to be designed for you.

There are, however, some supplements that tend to have an affect on most individuals and can be used regardless of your nutritional status. L-Theanine, an extract from green tea, is one of those grabbing the attention of the health profession worldwide.

L-theanine

L-theanine is an amino acid commonly found in green tea which has been shown to reduce mental and physical stress, and induces a feeling of relaxation. It has also been shown to improve cognition and mood! Isn't that a perfect coffee substitute! Scientists are unsure of how L-theanine works, but it is thought to increase the level of GABA, serotonin and dopamine production. Research has also shown that L-theanine promotes alpha wave production in the brain (those are the relaxed brain waves).

L-theanine is a very safe remedy to use. Studies on test rats have shown that even repeated extremely high doses of L-theanine cause little to no harmful psychological or physical effects. In fact, L-theanine showed neuroprotective effects in one rat study.

L-theanine may help the body's immune response to infection. In a study published in 2003 it was shown that tea drinkers had up to five times higher production of anti-bacterial proteins than coffee drinkers. So, if you want to give coffee the boot, green tea may be your perfect substitute to give you that alertness without the negative effects of coffee.

L-Tryptophan

Tryptophan is an essential amino acid, meaning that it cannot be produced by the body and must be supplied by the diet. However, in some cases there may be a higher demand for this amino acid. L-Tryptophan is easily obtainable and fairly inexpensive dietary supplement available at most health food stores or online. The L-Tryptophan is best taken without protein which can hamper its absorption. It is used regularly in Canada, the Netherlands, the UK, Germany and France. There have been no reports of any serious or widespread health problems using supplemental Trypthophan.

Emotional Freedom Technique (EFT)

This book wouldn't be complete without talking about this very powerful therapy. I now have the privilege of working very closely with a very talented EFT practitioner, Moira McFadyen. On many occasions I have seen patients with long-standing emotional issues resolve these very quickly with this therapy. In fact, I heard a friend recently say that EFT achieved in one session what several years of counselling could not.

I asked Moira to write an explanation about EFT:

EFT is a wonderful technique for depression as it clears the bad emotions from the body. EFT works with two parts of the brain, the conscious and the subconscious. The conscious brain is what you plan your day with and is your every conscious thought. Your subconscious brain is your memory banks. It stores everything your five senses (touch, taste, smell, feel and hear), have recorded since the moment they formed in your mother's womb. It is your reference library and is accessed every second of every day as a guide.

The problem with the subconscious is that it can't determine good or bad, right or wrong. It just absorbs everything it is given as fact. This is where problems arise. It carries every trauma you have experienced, every negative message you were given, every emotional hurt, pain and grief that you have suffered. This can be the underlying cause of depression.

I often use the analogy of an emotional well to describe how EFT works. We all put our bad emotions into the well and keep the lid on because no-one likes to feel bad. However as time goes by the well starts to fill, it becomes harder and harder to keep that lid on and this when emotions start to overflow and depressive symptoms start to appear.

Emotional Freedom Technique helps you to empty that emotional well. It removes the emotional charge from the bad or hurtful memories and messages, and gradually this well starts to empty again.

We do this by means of tapping the meridian lines (energy channels in the body) while at the same time as addressing the negative emotion in the subconscious via a set-up statement. As the subconscious' purpose is to protect you, once it realizes that the negative emotion is hurting, not helping, it then releases it via your meridian lines.

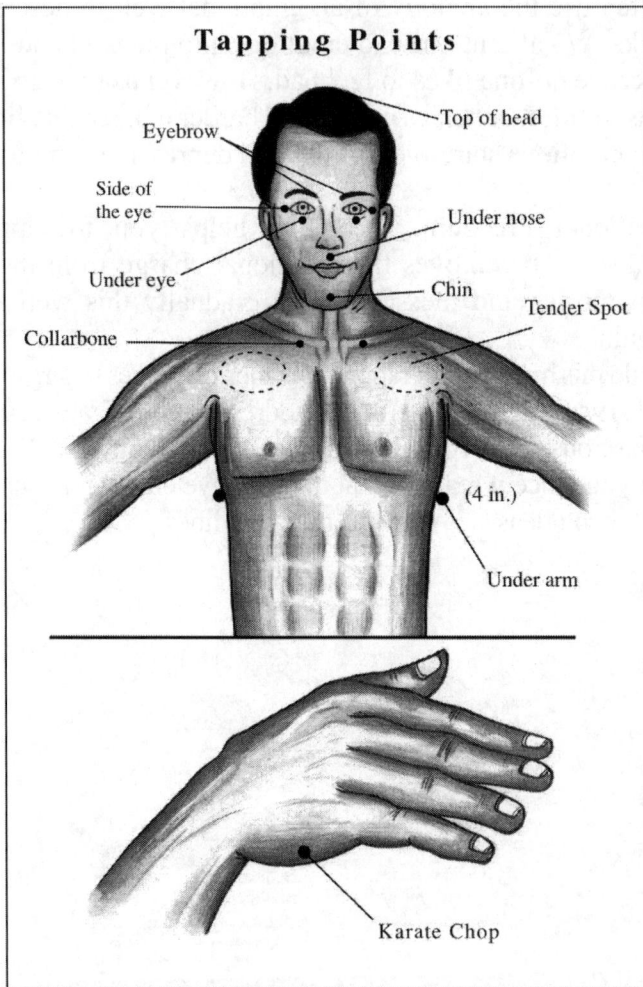

Image 7: The tapping chart

A good way to trial this is to use the Breath Technique. Please take a deep breath and then give yourself a number from 1 – 10 (1 being shallow breath, 10 full lung breath) and note this number down.

Now say the following set up statement while tapping on the karate chop points (side of the hand) with the four fingers of your other hand:

"Even though I have this tightness in my chest, maybe it is safe to relax and take a deep breath, and never-the-less I deeply and completely accept myself"

"Even though my rib cage feels a bit tight, maybe it is safe to relax and take a deep breath and never-the-less I deeply and completely accept myself"

"I would now like to total relax my diaphragm and take a deep breath in, it is safe to do so and never-the-less I deeply and completely accept myself.

Then tap each of the points on the chart, from the head down, slowly repeating the phrase "It is safe to take a deep breath".

Finally, take another deep breath in and give yourself another mark on a scale of 1 – 10. Pay attention to how you breathe and the depth of your breath. You should feel a beneficial difference.

EFT is a wonderful tool that can be used as a day to day coping mechanism or as a tool to remove really deep emotional issues.

Mary was a teenage girl who came to me with low self-esteem, stress/anxiety problem. She reported that she hadn't been sleeping properly and was constantly worrying about going home. She had moved to Britain from Australia 2 years before, but her family was now pressurizing her to go home as they were missing her. She confessed that she didn't want to see her mother, that they had never gotten on well and that she had been much happier being away from her. She could give me no reason for her feelings and just said that she had always felt like this. I spent time exploring Mary's childhood memories and tapping on the various negative messages she had received from her mother. She reported feeling calmer and a bit more optimistic. Suddenly she paused, looked surprised and said "I had totally forgotten about that". She then went on to tell me about a suppressed trauma memory.

When she was five she had witnessed a young boy drown in a swimming pool. She had seen his struggle, being dragged from the water and then his mother's grief as she realized he was dead. This had obviously traumatized Mary but upon returning to her family's caravan, her mother, who had no knowledge of what Mary had witnessed, shouted at her for being late for tea. The message Mary took from this incident was that her mother didn't love her. She had needed her mother's comfort but her mother had shouted at her instead. Children of that age expect their parents to know what they need, which is why Mary never told her mother what she had witnessed.

We then used EFT to 1) clear the trauma from Mary's body by tapping of all the aspects of what she had witnessed and 2) to reframe the message she had given herself about her mother's love. After the session Mary reported feeling "so much better". She emailed me two weeks later to thank me. She reported that she was feeling "so much better" and said that she had booked her flight home. She said that she had spoken to her mum on the phone and was now really looking forward to seeing her.

CHAPTER 7

Traditional Chinese Medicine and Acupuncture

As an acupuncturist, I may be biased when it comes to writing about Traditional Chinese Medicine (TCM) and Acupuncture. However, TCM has been around for more than 5000 years. It's an empirical science, which has developed from observing nature and the natural cycles of the world and although its principles are ancient, they are still relevant in today's world. As an acupuncturist, my goal is to nurture and support life, to encourage the flow of energy where blockages have arisen. It's a very different approach from Western medicine where it at times would appear that treating disease is a constant struggle. For instance, Western medicine talks about the fight against cancer or obesity, and medication names also give a hint to their actions: beta-blockers, antagonists etc.

TCM however, functions in a completely different way. We nourish and support the innate healing ability of the body. We encourage the individual to keep the body in equilibrium and balance.

Life according to TCM, unfolds from the dynamic equilibrium of two complementary forces, Yin and Yang. Although the energies of Yin and Yang are permanently changing, they are in a cycle of continuous movement, a graceful dance to sustain balance, or equilibrium.

Yin and Yang

To understand how TCM works, one has to understand the concept that underlies TCM theory.

According to TCM, everything in nature can be characterized as either Yin or Yang. The Chinese characters for Yin and Yang depict the shady and sunny sides of a mountain respectively. Although they are considered opposites, they are complementary and mutually depend on one another. Yin and Yang are rooted in one another; they are interdependent and inseparable, yet they are relative to one another. Yin cannot exist without Yang as Yang cannot exist without Yin. Without darkness, there is no light. Without stillness, there is no movement. The image below beautifully represents the continuous flow between Yin and Yang. We can also see that within each energy lies the seed of its opposite, emphasizing their interdependence. For instance, within stillness (Yin) there lies the capacity to transform into movement (Yang).

Ying & Yang

Image 8: The dance of Yin and Yang

In the Chinese medical system, the physiology and anatomy of the body is considered a delicate dance between the Yin and Yang functions within the body. When Yin and Yang are in balance, we are calm, focused, centered, in control and the emotions and body flow naturally, without illness. Any disruption to the balance of these

Yin and Yang

- When Yin and Yang are balanced the mind is calm and settled
- Yin deficiencies result in agitation, nervousness and unease
- Yang deficiencies result in indecisiveness, stagnation, inability to express needs and hopelessness

energies, however, will result in symptoms in the mind, emotions and body.

The Yin qualities in the body sustain us, root us and enable us to rest and contemplate. When there is sufficient Yin energy, the person is content, receptive and settled. Insufficient Yin, however, results in agitation, nervousness and a feeling of unease.

By contrast, Yang enables change and transformation, spurring us on to react, respond and actively engage in life. When Yang is insufficient, the power of movement is lost and we feel paralyzed by fear, indecisive, stagnated, hopeless and unable to express our needs.

Qi

Qi (pronounced 'chee') is the vital energy that runs through all of us, giving us the breath of life. It is an active energy that enables the movement function within the body, i.e. transportation of nutrients, movement of the muscles, functioning of the physical organs and the mind. It also involves our defences to the outside world, both physically (e.g. from viruses), emotionally and mentally (e.g. negative energy). Qi needs to flow freely throughout the body to perform its functions, if it becomes stagnated, certain functions; both physically and mentally will be affected. Repressed emotion that has no release, especially frustration and anger, tends to cause Qi to become stagnated.

Qi
▪ The vital energy that results in life
▪ Provides our defences to the outside world both physically and mentally

An acupuncturist would for instance treat depressive symptoms according to the whole pattern. For instance, a patient with depression accompanied by outbursts of anger, bloating and migratory pains will be treated for Qi stagnation. While another patient with depression may have weakness, lowered sex drive and motivation and in this case the acupuncturist would work to increase Yin.

The Foundation of the mind in Traditional Chinese Medicine

In order to understand depression and anxiety from a Traditional Chinese Medicine (TCM) perspective it is necessary to explain how the 'Mind' is formed. It is thought that the "Mind" of a baby is created from the union of the "Essence" (genetic make-up) of the mother and father. Essence is similar to the genetic concept, where the sperm meets the egg and a genetic union takes place. What TCM calls "Essence" is a rough equivalent of our DNA make-up or genetic inheritance.

At conception the Essence of the mother combines with the Essence of the father to form the mind (Shen) of the baby. In one of the Chinese medical classics called the Spiritual Axis, it reads: "Life comes about through the Essence; when the two Essences (of mother and father) unite, they form the mind."

The Chinese character for 'Essence' (Jing) is a combination of two characters: 'rice' and 'refined'. So, this precious substance can be considered the product of a process of refinement or distillation and is something to be cherished and guarded.

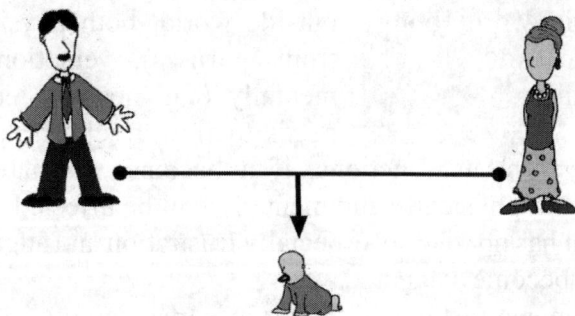

Prenatal essence which forms the basis of the 'Mind' of the baby

It is this union of this essence which establishes the prenatal essence of the baby giving us our basic constitutional strength and vitality. It is 'Essence', or our genetic fingerprint, that makes each of us unique. As with genetics, this substance is fixed and cannot be greatly influenced later in life. It is for this reason that Essence is considered the foundation of the mind. From a TCM point of view,

Essence can be compared to the Genes part of the formula that was discussed in Chapter 3.

The formula shows all the contributing factors that make up your "stress tolerance" or basal stress response.

$$\text{Genes} + \text{early adversity} + \text{nutrition} + \text{environment} + \text{trauma} = \text{basal stress response}$$

The TCM concept is not very different from what science is unearthing now. Numerous studies have shown that our behaviour and personality is partly genetic. We also know that many mental heath disorders, such as schizophrenia, are linked to alterations at specific chromosomes on the genetic map.

Western and Chinese medicine are singing from the same sheet when it comes to Genes or Essence. But, it gets more complicated. It is true that we mostly "inherit" the mind from our parents, but this is not just through the genetic fingerprint or 'Essence' from the parents. TCM strongly believes that the biological foundation of the mind is a combination of our genetic lottery (Essence) as well as the condition of our parents' state of health at the time of conception and the mother's health during pregnancy. In other words, if your parents

> The biological foundation of the mind is a combination of our genetic lottery (Essence) as well the conditions of our parents' state of health during pregnancy.

were healthy at the time of conception you would receive a healthy set of genes and your mind would have a strong foundation. However, during pregnancy and after birth, the nutrition and emotional environment would add or subtract to this foundation, either strengthening or weakening the mind.

This is where TCM differentiates between prenatal Essence and postnatal Essence. To roughly equate the Western and Eastern concept, Prenatal Essence can be likened to the DNA contributed by mother and father as well as the health of the mother during pregnancy. Postnatal essence involves all the factors that will influence Essence after the birth. Although DNA (and prenatal Essence) is fixed and cannot be easily influenced later in life, the Postnatal Essence can, and so TCM places emphasis on changing the conditions that you can change. Traditionally in China young couples trying to conceive would make sure that they are in the best state of health possible so as to positively influence the pre-natal Essence of the baby. After the birth, the mother would nourish herself and the baby to strengthen the post-natal essence. This is believed to create a strong mind for the baby later in life.

So, the mind is already formed "genetically", which can be considered our mental constitution. If the Essence of both the mother and father is healthy at the time of conception, the mind of the baby will flourish, be balanced, calm and alert. If Essence is depleted or compromised, the mind suffers and there is a tendency for depression or anxiety later in life. Nourishment during pregnancy and breastfeeding is also vital as any deficiencies will result in a depleted "Essence" and so TCM places great importance on the diet of the pregnant and breastfeeding mother. In fact, in China, there are special 'medicinal' dishes that are made up and served to women who are pregnant or breastfeeding. This is a TCM concept has been embraced culturally and is still very much practiced in China today.

Very importantly, the theory then expands to say that postnatal conditions are critical to the development of the mind. So, although our genes are fixed, there are more factors that come into play to determine our mental outlook. This includes nutrition as well as stress or early trauma. Poor nutrition or trauma in early life can lead to an anxious or depressed disposition later on in life and especially so if there is already a genetic weakness (weak Essence). The opposite is also true. If given the right nutrition, even a genetic weakness leading to anxiety or depression can be overcome. So, we can see that the TCM theory is not much different from the formula now supported in modern medicine:

Genes + early adversity + nutrition + environment + trauma = basal stress response.

Both theories, one a modern western hypothesis and the other an ancient eastern concept are in essence saying the same thing. Our genes (or Essence) together with nutritional factors during the very early development of the foetus gives us our mental predisposition (basal stress response). TCM classics also emphasise that we cannot change the disposition that was given to us at birth, but we can give the mind the nourishment that it needs (nutritionally and emotionally) to keep the mind as happy and balanced given our dispositions.

> For those who have not been dealt a good hand of cards early in life, taking the extra effort to nourish the mind is an absolute essential

For those, then, who have not been dealt a good hand of cards in early life, taking the extra effort to nourish the mind is an absolute essential. Physicians in China place special emphasis on this and encourage patients to actively manage their own health so as to preserve their mental health. The fundamental principles they will teach their patients is to maintain a sense of balance.

Since TCM theory arose from closely observing the natural rhythms and patterns of our world. If we follow the example and cues of nature, we can get many clues on how to bring our bodies into harmony with nature. When we are in tune with nature on a physical and spiritual level, we can find harmony and balance within ourselves (both physically and mentally).

Mental Health: keeping the balance

Balance and moderation are one of the most vital elements of traditional Chinese systems. It can be a difficult concept for westerners to grasp as we tend to take things to the extreme. I see patients daily who have decided to tackle a health problem and then "go at it" with all cylinders blasting. These are the patients coming in who plan to get this problem sorted, one way or another.

This brings to mind a female patient, Liz, who consulted me about a walking problem. Since childhood Liz had struggled to walk, having to use a stick and always being very conscious of her walking. No physical reason had ever been found for her limp and doctors had decided that her problem was psychosomatic. She agreed that the she was so consciously aware of her walking and felt continuously judged by others. She lacked confidence in her own ability to walk. When she finally made the decision to do something about it, she took it to the extreme.

She started acupuncture, Pilates, physiotherapy, tai chi and relaxation tapes all at once. She became obsessive about her treatments, therapies and exercises. Her entire day and weeks were now focused on the 'problem'. Not surprisingly, her walking got worse. She had focused all her energy and attention on solving the problem.

I am not at all saying that we should ignore our problems and do nothing about them. We do have to take responsibility for our own conditions. I am only saying that moderation and balance is necessary. When Liz' physiotherapist pointed out to her that she is maybe focusing too much on the problem, she decided to balance her healing programme out with some other distractions and relaxed a little more about the 'problem'. Her walking very quickly responded and improved.

In all things in life, balance and moderation is the key. While we do have to take action to put the right things in place, we also need to sometimes "let go" to naturally allow the body to heal. It reminds me of my very dear patient Judy who always says: "We are human beings. Not human doings!"

In fact, it is thought that extremes are the cause of most illnesses in TCM. TCM physicians will tell you that all energies and nutrients are needed in moderation. We need sugar, but too much will cause weakness to the Spleen (or pancreas) leading to diabetes. Sex is necessary for the beneficial exchange of energy between Yin and Yang, but excessive sex is thought to deplete the Essence. Overeating or under-eating can damage the health. Overwork or its opposite, inactivity, as well as excessive emotions (such as constant anger) are also causes of disease.

So, how can we achieve balance? The practice of Tai Chi and Qigong were originally developed to help maintain balance on the mental, physical and emotional level. These practices teach the individual how to balance out energy in the body so as to keep the emotions and physical body in harmony. A healthy mind depends also on the strength of the post-natal Essence, which is generated by our nutritional intake. For this reason, we will talk very briefly about the TCM diet.

Post-natal Essence: The TCM diet

We now understand why engendering Post-natal essence is essential for anyone with mental health concerns. There is little that we can do about our genetic pre-disposition, but we can strengthen the Post-natal Essence, thus building a robust mind.

One of the fundamental TCM principles states that if the Stomach and intestines are well nourished and in good health, the mental activity is stable and the mind flourishes. If, however, the gut is compromised, the mind becomes depressed, anxious and cloudy. The health of the gut is a fundamental concern in treating any mental health conditions in TCM. The state of mind, however, also affects the gut and so continuous stress or overwork is thought to damage the digestive system.

"if the stomach and intestines are well nourished and in good health, the mental activity is stable and the mind flourishes. If, however, the gut is compromised, the mind becomes depressed, anxious and cloudy"

Although the theory is a lot more complex, any acupuncturist will tell you that the physiological health of the body has an indissoluble relationship with the state of the mind, in the same way that the state of mind will affect the organs.

The 5 elements and the TCM Diet

One of the fundamental theories in TCM nutrition is the five elements which follow the seasonal cycles. The five elements are Water, Fire, Wood, Metal and Earth. The elements symbolize natural phenomena and qualities or processes. Wood (Spring) is the start of the cycle and corresponds to spring and birth, Fire (summer) to rapid growth and expansion, Earth (late summer) to transformation, Metal (autumn) to the harvest and Water (winter) to storage.

Physiologically, the interplay of all the elements; their balance and interactions create harmony or disharmony within the body (and nature as a whole). As the elements also represent specific emotions TCM practitioners aim to create a balance between the elements (or energies) in order to create harmonious emotions.

	Wood	**Fire**	**Earth**	**Metal**	**Water**
Season	Spring	Summer	Late summer	Autumn	Winter
Development	Birth	Growth	Transformation	Harvest	Storage
Organs	Liver & Gall Bladder	Heart & Small Intestine	Spleen & Stomach	Lungs & Large Intestine	Kidneys & Bladder
Emotions	Anger	Joy	Pensiveness	Sadness	Fear
Tastes	Sour	Bitter	Sweet	Pungent	Salty

The elements are qualities that help explain the connections and interactions between the organ systems in TCM. In what is called the generating sequence, each element is generated by one and generates another. Thus, Fire generates Earth, Earth generates Metal, Metal generates Water, Water generates Wood and Wood generates fire. The elements also 'control' one another in order to create balance. For instance, Earth controls Water, Wood controls Earth.

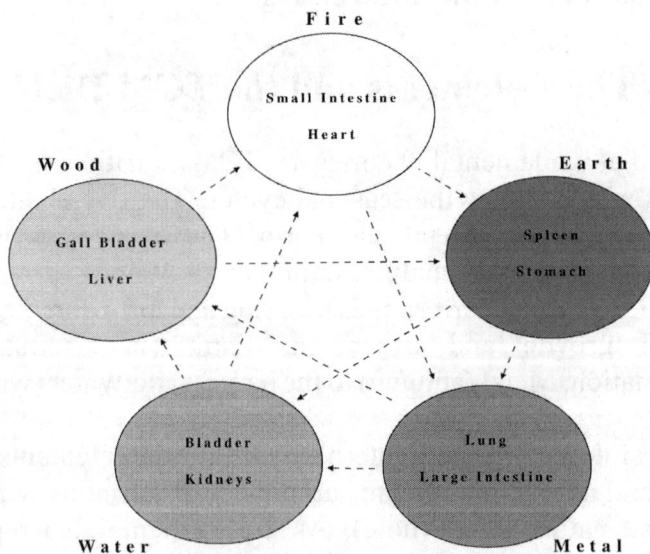

Image 8: The five elements

The generating and controlling sequences is a way of self-regulating the energy within the body and also nature on a larger scale. In Chinese dietary practice, to balance out the elements patients are advised to eat foods from all the tastes, not favouring or avoiding any one taste. Chinese dinner tables are always balanced with salty, sweet, sour, bitter and pungent foods. In the West, however, we have largely excluded some tastes (especially bitter) and over-eat sweet and salty foods leading to imbalance in the elements. In other cases, salt is completely avoided because of its bad press. Although TCM dietary concepts support the theory that too much salt (Water) damages the Heart (Fire), it is only when in excess. A small amount of salt is needed to support Kidney and adrenal function.

If imbalance creeps into the system, one element may over-control or suppress another and the relationships among them break down leading to one Element being in excess in relation to another. When energy imbalances occur, illness or dis-ease follows.

Practitioners will often use this system to determine if there are any energy imbalances and will, in addition to using acupuncture to balance and shift the energy, make lifestyle recommendations. For instance, a person with an over-active Wood element may have an excess of Anger emotionally. A TCM practitioner would advise them to avoid pungent and sour foods (such garlic, onion, vinegar and citrus) which further agitate this element. Since Wood controls Earth, the sweet taste would be beneficial to the Liver (but once again in moderation!)

The theory gets a lot more complicated and it isn't always easy to determine which element you may need. However, if you keep your food balanced, adding in a little of each taste with every meal you will help to re-establish the balance.

The mind-gut connection in TCM

Very early in embryonic development the gut and the brain develop from the same embryonic tissue. Later, when it divides, one part will grow into the central nervous system (brain and cranial nerves) and the other the enteric nervous system (the gut brain). The gut brain or enteric nervous system is a sheath of nerves lining the whole of the gut, with more than one hundred million neurotransmitters lining the length of the gut. The same neurotransmitters that affect the brain affect the gut and visa versa.

It is not surprising then that TCM places very strong emphasis on gut health when treating any mental-emotional conditions. Most often, the following organs are often implicated and treated when any mental or emotional conditions show.

- Stomach
- Spleen
- Small Intestine
- Large Intestine
- Liver

Although these are by far not the only causes of mental imbalance in TCM, they do play a significant role in treatment. They also help us to understand how very important diet is in the conquering mental conditions.

The Stomach:

The Stomach has a place of special importance in TCM theory. It is known as the 'Root of the Postnatal Essence'. It is the vesicle that receives food and is referred to often as the "Great Granary'. The Stomach has the function of transforming the food that it receives through a process of fermentation providing nourishment for the both the physical and mental. Preserving the Stomach energy (or Qi) is one of the most important functions to both physical and mental health.

If the Stomach is strong and has enough Qi to extract nutrients from the food the person will feel strong and full of vitality. If it fails in its function, the body and brain does not receive vital nutrients and the person will feel tired and possibly depressed. In order to establish the health of the Stomach, TCM practitioners look at the coating of the tongue. A thin white coating on the tongue is indicative of good Stomach function. The absence of any coating indicates that the Stomach's function is impaired. Thick coatings (either yellow or white) also show dysfunction of this organ.

The Stomach dislikes receiving food late at night and so mealtimes should be early, preferably no later than 7pm. There is a good reason for this. The body has a natural circadian cycle which enables the organs shut-down and repair time. If you think of a factory that has a production line running 24/7, there is usually scheduled maintenance on certain areas of production at specific times of the day. In the same way, each organ has its scheduled repair time when its function is minimal enabling repair to take place. Each organ also has its peak functioning time when it's working to its full capacity.

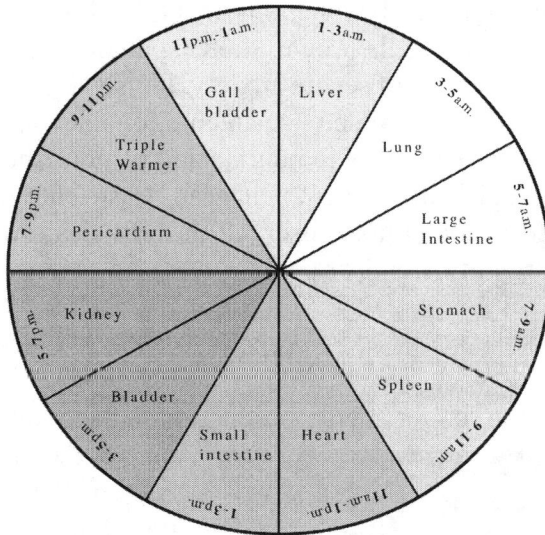

The horary clock in TCM

As you can see from the horary cycle, Stomach function peaks between 7 and 9am in the morning, but it has its repair and shut down time between 7 and 9pm in the evening. Eating heavy meals late at night will place more stress on the Stomach, interfering with it its critical repair time.

- Eating late at night harms the function of the Stomach
- Stomach dysfunction manifests with tiredness, withdrawal from the world, severe anxiety and mild depression
- A lack of nourishment on an emotional level contributes to Stomach pathology

The Stomach influences the mental state in TCM directly by providing nutrients required for optimal brain function but it also through its connection with the Vagus nerve. As the foetus develops, cells are rapidly dividing and differentiating into all the bits that the body needs. One specific clump of cells will initially grow together but as the foetus develops, it will go on to divide, forming the brain and the gut, remaining closely connected by the Vagus nerve. The fact that these two systems share the same early cell lines mean that they are closely connected.

When the Stomach dysfunctions, mentally this manifests with a person wanting to be on their own, shutting themselves off from the world and with feelings of severe anxiety. Physically the person will feel tired and mildly depressed. On an emotional level, the Stomach can be harmed by our ability to nourish and be nourished. A lack of emotional or spiritual nourishment can contribute to Stomach pathology and is sometimes observed in individuals who lack the nurturing energy of parents or perhaps were 'over-nurtured'.

Spleen:

The Spleen is the root of energy production in the body. The Spleen houses the intellect and is responsible for memory, concentration, studying and ideas. The Spleen becomes weakened by pensiveness and worry, but at the same time, these thought patterns are a symptom of a weak Spleen. In severe cases, a feeble Spleen will generate obsessive thinking.

- The Spleen is responsible for memory, focus, concentration, ideas
- Pensiveness and worry affects the Spleen
- Obsessive thinking is linked to the Spleen

The Spleen belongs to the Earth element, which is the centre point of all the elements, and so it is thought that if the Earth element, and thus Spleen energy is wavering, the person loses their centre, causing the individual to feel depressed and lack confidence. The Spleen is very much affected by the diet, and is very sensitive to nutritional deficiencies or insults. The Spleen dislikes dairy, cold foods and sugar. So for those with difficulty in concentration or obsessive thinking, a dairy free diet is essential!

Small Intestine

The Small Intestine has the function of receiving food from the
Stomach and processing
it, separating it into clear
nutritive fluid and turbid
waste. In the same way,

- Helps to discriminate between issues

on a mental level, it enables us to separate issues, being able to
discriminate what course of action to take. The Small Intestine is
closely related to the Heart and is therefore often considered in the
treatment of depression when there is lack of clarity in decision
making.

Large Intestine

The main function of the Large Intestine is to receive food and fluid
from the Small Intestine,
absorb the nutrients and
fluids, and excrete the
waste. On a mental

- Helps to push through and achieve
- Helps resolve stagnated grief

level, the Large Intestine is often linked with determination and the
focus to push through difficulties until success is gained. When an
individual has dreams and ambitions, but cannot succeed in making
them a reality the Large Intestine must be considered. Also, in cases
where an individual holds on to a grief pattern for longer than is
healthy. Of course, grieving is a normal response to loss but when but
when the emotions are still all consuming many years later and one is
stuck grief, the addition of Large Intestine points can help.

TCM is exceptionally complex and to try and explain the theory
in this book would not be justified. I have, however, included some
examples of the symptoms in some of the pattern discriminations that
relate to depression and anxiety. This is by no means an exhaustive
list and is only for the interest of the reader.

The gut, however, is not the only contributor to mental
imbalance according to TCM. Because it is a holistic system, a
dysbalance in any of the organs can contribute to depression and
anxiety. Other organs that play a role in the function of the mind
include the Heart, Kidneys, Liver and Gall Bladder.

Deficiency patterns

- **Heart deficiency** Restlessness, anxiety, weepiness, frequent yawning, a pale tongue with thin white fur and a fine pulse.
- **Heart and Spleen deficiency** Over-thinking, worry, palpitations, poor sleep, poor memory, lack of concentration, depression, weak limbs and fatigue.
- **Spleen and Kidney Yang deficiency** Depression, wanting to sleep but sleep disturbed, impotence in men, worry, anxiety, absent or decreased libido, lower back pain, cold feet and a fat pale tongue with teeth-marked edges.
- **Yin deficiency with raging fire** Dizziness, heart palpitations, poor sleep, easily angered, lower back pain, menstrual irregularities in women, anxiety, a red tongue, agitation and depression.
- **Heart-Spleen deficiency** Over-thinking with a tendency to worry, heart palpitations, poor sleep quality, poor memory, lack of concentration, fatigue and lack of strength in the limbs.

Excess patterns

- **Liver stagnation** Irritability, premenstrual breast distension, hormonal imbalance, when depressed avoids people and does not want to talk.
- **Liver depression and heat** Anger, tinnitus, headache, and constipation in addition to the Liver Stagnation symptoms.
- **Liver blood stasis** Agitation, depression, suicidal thoughts, painful menstruation and choppy pulse
- **Phlegm fire harassing the Spirit** Insomnia, tight feeling in the head, acid regurgitation, nausea, vertigo and dizziness, anxiety and restlessness

The next section, Emotional Healing, also describes how TCM connects the emotions and mental and physical health.

Patients who have had successful treatment often wonder why there are not more studies showing the effectiveness of acupuncture, and I always explain that research studies are designed to treat a specific condition, and do not allow for the individuality of treatment that is the base of acupuncture! Universities and research groups are, however, now beginning to recognise that the research structure does not fit with alternative medicine, and are finding ways to positively change the way in which research is carried out.

Acupuncture has a number of proven beneficial physiological effects – its relaxation response has been shown to decrease the heart rate, lower blood pressure and produce a calming or tranquilizing action. Acupuncture can relieve feelings of anxiety and depression and can give a person a feeling of well-being and self-confidence. It is an effective substitute for sleeping pills, tranquilizers and antidepressant drugs. Acupuncture can be used in many cases not only as an alternative to these drugs but also to treat side effects and dependence. In fact, a number of patients who come in for acupuncture treatment do so specifically to come off their antidepressants. There is considerable evidence that acupuncture could substantially reduce the consumption of drugs such as Prozac.

Although it cannot, of course, change life circumstances, it can create a feeling of well-being and confidence, giving the person the ability to cope with aspects of his/her life situation, and make the necessary changes that may be needed.

It usually takes 6-8 acupuncture sessions to reach the same effect as anti-depressants or anti-anxiety medications. In some cases, it can take a little longer if there are more complicated patterns involved. Acupuncture is virtually painless. The needles are so thin that several acupuncture needles can go into the middle of a hypodermic needle. Occasionally, there is a brief moment of discomfort as the needle penetrates the skin, but once the needles are in place, most people relax and even fall asleep for the duration of the treatment.

To find a practitioner in the UK you can contact the British Acupuncture Council (www.**acupuncture**.org.uk) and check with the practitioner whether they have experience in treating mental health issues.

Qigong

I discovered Qigong quite by accident several years ago. I was at a course which required us to learn Qigong (much to my annoyance). I had enrolled for a master's degree in Acupuncture and was interested in the academic knowledge I would gain. I did not see how learning exercises held any relevance for me. However, the experiences that arose from the course created a curiosity in me. The deeper I dug, the more I practiced and the more people I spoke with, I became increasingly convinced that I had stumbled onto something quite remarkable and very powerful.

One woman on the course had been in the middle of a very traumatic separation from her husband while at the same time coping with the death of her father. Lizzy was anxious and suffering from very severe depression. Somewhere in the middle of the course, at the end of two days of very intensive practice, Lizzy had transformed into a sparkling, bright woman. Her drawn features had disappeared and most noticeably she had transformed from a nervous, depressed and insecure woman to a glowing and happy being. I am still in contact with Lizzy and the changes that began over those two days have remained with her, and so has her Qigong practice.

When anxiety and depression manifests as a result of energy flow imbalance, Qigong can be remarkably powerful. Not everyone will experience such a rapid transformation as Lizzy, but with steady and committed practice, slow and steady progress is guaranteed. Having worked with many people who are committed to Qigong practice, I can now confidently say that Qigong must be the most powerful anti-depressant and anti-anxiety remedy I have ever encountered. The term Qigong roughly translates to the "practice or cultivation" of Qi. Through using posture, movement and breath, this form of exercise has evolved alongside TCM for over 5000 years. Today, many hospitals in China use Qigong for a variety of ailments.

Qigong is a very gentle practice and because of that I found it difficult to understand how it could have any effect. I could comprehend how strenuous physical exercise may have an effect on the body but I was curious about how these seemingly simple exercises could affect the mind. It seemed odd to me that repeating certain gentle movements would have such a remarkable effect.

One of my teachers, Peter Deadman, explained that the Qigong exercises create coherence between the Jing (dense physical body), Qi and Shen (volatile spirit/consciousness). Correct movement and posture (Jing), leads to free flow of Qi. When the Qi flows freely and without resistance, the Shen (spirit) is balanced. Unlike aerobics or gym workouts, Qigong's focus is not solely on creating physical strength. Qigong's goal is to create harmony between mind, body and spirit and that makes it very relevant in mental and spiritual health.

Kenneth Cohen in his book *The Way of Qigong* explains that Qigong theory takes into account how the emotions affect posture, breathing and organ health. By shifting current energy blockages that present as a result of pent up emotions, it is possible to dissipate psychological problems. Because the body stores emotional memory in the physical body, through specific movements and breathe-work it is possible to free many trapped emotions.

Interesting research has emerged in the past few years that confirm the effectiveness of Qigong in dealing with depression. I cannot think of a more natural and powerful way of healing the body and mind.

CHAPTER 8

Emotional well-being

There is increasing data showing that when we assume an emotional state, it triggers our internal chemistry, and the way in which information is passed through our cells (using tiny electrical vibrations). If you are aware of your emotions, you can often physically feel your emotions in different regions of your body. That is because the cellular receptors (which are like locks and keys) are scattered throughout the body. I know that I've had more physical pain from a loved one's rejection than from when I recovered from surgery!

Sayings like "that guy that is a pain in the neck" or "this really galls me" makes the point. In fact, when you are in a state of mind where you are holding grudges or brooding about issues in the past, it will also change the body and mind chemistry leading to ill health in time. I often find that looking at the physical side of depression or anxiety is not enough. Emotional and spiritual healing is just as vital to bringing about healing.

One of the most powerful emotions that enables healing is the ability to forgive. Forgiveness means untying yourself from the emotions and thoughts that bind you to the offence committed against you. In doing so, you reduce the feelings that have a hold over you, and thus become freer. Forgiving not just others but also ourselves is one of the most powerful vehicles for healing. I have seen many debilitating health conditions turn around when forgiveness came into play.

Forgiveness does not mean condoning or forgetting what has been done. In fact, the act that hurt you will always remain a part of your life. Forgiveness, however, is about lessening the hold that this act has on you to free you up emotionally. This does not mean that you deny, condone or minimise the act. It is possible to forgive the other person without excusing what they have done.

Researchers have recently become interested in studying the effects of forgiveness. More recently there is evidence that holding on to grudges and bitterness results in long-term health problems. Forgiveness, on the other hand, offers numerous benefits, such as lowering blood pressure, depression and anxiety! In order to heal ourselves, we must forgive.

It is often those close to us that can hurt us the most (including ourselves). When you are hurt by someone's actions or words, intentional or not, you may begin experiencing negative feelings such as anger, confusion or sadness. These feelings may start out small, but can grow if you don't deal with them quickly. They may even begin to crowd out positive feelings. Grudges filled with resentment, vengeance and hostility take root when you dwell on hurtful events or situations, replaying them in your mind many times.

So, how do we forgive? Forgiveness is a commitment to a process of change. It's not a one-time event, and it can be difficult and it does take time. Firstly, you must recognise the value of forgiveness and its importance in your life. You must also realise that forgiveness is something that you do for **yourself** and not the other person. Consider how holding onto this grudge has affected your life and well-being. Then, actively choose to forgive the one who has offended you. In this way, you move away from your role as a victim, and release the control and power the offending person and situation have had in your life. As you forgive, you will naturally let go of hostility, resentment and misery; which then makes way for compassion, kindness and peace.

Keeping our emotions in balance is not always easy in this demanding world that we live in. However, we can learn to use our emotions as radars that quickly pick up when things are going wrong. Addressing these emotions as they arise will help keep us on track physically, mentally and spiritually.

One story that comes to mind is a young gentleman I saw a few years ago. Michael had been suffering from quite severe depression which was unresponsive to a battery of anti-depressants. After talking with Michael for a while, we got to the bottom of why he felt depressed. A few years prior, Michael had met a women who he fell deeply in love with which resulted in an extra-marital affair. He felt extreme guilt as his religion did not make divorce an option for him. Michael ended the affair and chose to remain with his family. He desperately wanted to rebuild the crumbling relationship with his wife. The guilt of what he had done remained with him and he eventually developed severe depression. At the point where I had seen Michael, he had lost his job because the depression had crippled him and he couldn't face going into work. This in turn placed more pressure on his marriage and his role in the family.

We spoke for a while about why it was important for him to forgive himself. Michael felt that he deserved his current situation, and that his depression was his rightful punishment for letting his family down. He suggested that the way he felt inside was justified punishment for what he had done. I pointed out that he was in fact punishing his entire family through this depression, and that it was not helping the family he had wanted to protect. We spoke about forgiveness, and how it would be possible for him to forgive himself (which is not the same as condoning what he had done) so that he could rebuild his family life. He had to forgive himself for the sake of his family's happiness.

To be honest, Michael could not accept this immediately, and I would not be telling the truth if I said that the next time I saw him, the issue was resolved. It took Michael a few months and small increments of forgiveness before he came to terms with what had happened. He worked hard at consciously forgiving himself. Now, I can happily report that Michael does have a happy family life, has rebuilt the relationship with his wife and is depression-free!

Anxiety and depression can often be indicators that there is something wrong in our lives that need fixing. Just like indicators in a car, they can tell us ahead of time of things that need to be taken care of. If you ignore the messages, you're likely to keep going for a little while, but at some point you will run out of fuel! By looking at what our triggers are, we can try and find the cause of the anxiety or depression. This isn't always easy to do. Sometimes a relationship needs work or changing, a job may need changing, or sometimes it's as simple as speaking up about something you've not had the courage to do so before, in order that healing can take place.

Emotions, mind, Spirit and Traditional Chinese Medicine (TCM)

The subject of psychoneuroimmunology is gaining more attention as science begins to unravel the mystery of the connections between the brain, endocrine, immune and nervous systems. Although the link between emotions, hormones and neuropeptides is not yet fully understood, there is convincing evidence that emotions have a powerful effect on health and visa versa.

Chinese Medicine has for more than 5000 years studied emotions as being causes of disease, and has documented ideas of how emotions can lead to physical symptoms. TCM practitioners acknowledge underlying emotional causes in disease and will treat the person accordingly. Thoughts and emotions can influence the glands, the immune system, the autonomic nervous system, the skin, muscles, intestines, heart, circulation and breathing.

The physical symptoms that result from emotional causes are the body's way of communicating to us to resolve certain issues. It is therefore important for us to learn to recognize our emotions, and listen to their messages, so that we can use them in a positive, constructive and non-damaging way.

Emotions as cause of disease

We have to deal with emotions every day, and under normal circumstances they are not a cause of disease. We cannot avoid being angry, sad, afraid or aggrieved in the course of our lives. The death of somebody close to us, for example, will naturally provoke grief. However, emotions only become the cause of disease when they are excessive or prolonged. If a person is constantly angry about something for many years, this emotion will definitely lead to disease. In fact, many emotions are considered healthy, and provide us the mental energy and determination to go through life. For instance, anger can make us stronger and more determined when fighting for a specific cause.

In TCM it is believed that the way we manage emotions make them either harmful or beneficial to ourselves. Anger, for instance, can be either dissipated in an outburst of fury, or it can be harnessed to provide the courage and drive to achieve goals. So, learning to recognise and acknowledge emotions can help us in healing.

In TCM, emotions are believed to create an energetic resonance which influences our health. If we can harness the power of our emotions, we are able to bring about physical healing!

Anger affecting the Liver

This includes resentment, frustration, bitterness and a feeling of thwarted desires. The effect of anger will depend on the person's reaction to external stimulus The symptoms usually show in the head and neck: headaches, tinnitus, dizziness and a red face. Often when people are frustrated, they may end up drinking alcohol which is very toxic to the liver. This may create short-term relaxation, but the Liver will suffer more as a result.

Repressed anger, however, can often appear as a depression. This usually happens when it is not appropriate to show anger, usually to someone in authority. The person may show all the signs of depression, such as losing interest in life, but it's like a volcano waiting to erupt. In these cases, there are usually liver symptoms accompanying the depression, such as swollen and tender breasts and PMS in women, headaches or hypertension. It goes both ways, TCM also believes that a liver imbalance can cause anger and depression, and in this case it's the physiological change that results in the felt emotions.

These symptoms are messages from our organs, and in this case one is recommended to:

- nurture the liver with herbs such as milk thistle
- find a constructive outlet for the anger, such as sport or exercise
- address the underlying cause of the anger, such as learning to be more assertive. A good acupressure point to massage to release anger is Liver 3 (Liv3):

To locate Liv3, run your index finger along the space between the first and second toe. About a thumb width from the web you will find a hollow depression. Massage this point for 1-2 minutes each day with a deep pressure.

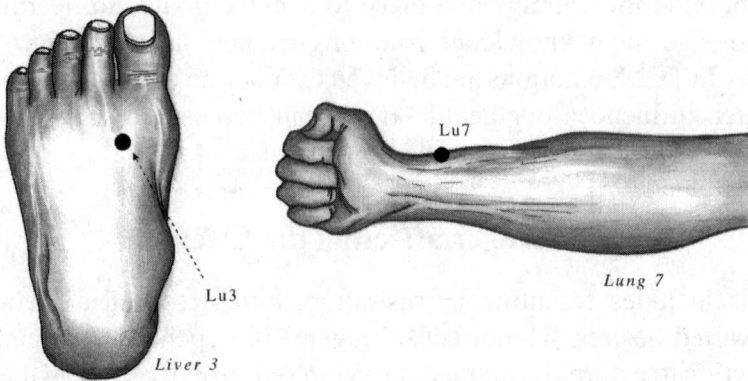

Image 9: Liv3 and Lu7

This brings to mind a patient who came into the clinic with severe and chronic pain in the area of the Liver. He had become a heavy drinker to ease the abdominal pain, which was growing worse each day. It emerged that he had a long-term repressed anger towards his boss which needed to be addressed. A short course of acupuncture, milk thistle, forgiveness and taking up running enabled the pain to ease within a very short period of time.

Craving affects the Heart

Excess craving and always wanting more is considered harmful for the heart. This is very common in today's pressured society where we have so many options available to us. In the past, men (or women) would be born in a village, and their life path would be laid out for them. To survive, they would have very little option but to remain in the village, follow the profession of their ancestors, and stay within the cultural restraints of society. They knew exactly what was expected of them.

In our modern society, however, children grow up with so many options available to them. We are told that we can be whatever we desire: astronauts, engineers, artists, etc. We have choices about where we want to live, which religious beliefs we want to follow, which social opinions we support, etc. This surplus of opportunity comes with a price of stress. It creates an inner voice which is never satisfied; always demanding more than we can give.

Suddenly, we could all be overnight stars on the X Factor. Our destinies are ours and the pressure in society is on to achieve something great. No wonder our society now has more heart disease! According to TCM, some of the physical symptoms that go along with this include: palpitations, over-excitability, insomnia and restlessness.

There are many classical Chinese medical texts that warn against excessive desires. Leading a simple life and moving your focus to spiritual growth is the best remedy. In this way, breathing techniques, tai chi and Qi gong can be very useful. This does not mean we should be without ambition. There is nothing unhealthy about wanting more from life. Being hopeful about health, finances and relationships is, in itself, healing. It is the negative dwelling on the things that we don't have, and not being satisfied with what we do have, that is harmful.

Keeping a gratitude diary where we note down all the little things we can be thankful for can be a powerful way to keep us from excessively desiring more. Keeping notes of the things that we are grateful for, such as having a family or even just having a warm place to sleep at night, can help to put things into perspective when we feel we are not getting what we deserve from life. Getting involved in voluntary community work also helps us move the focus away from what we want and need and can be very medicinal.

The point to affect cravings is Heart 7 (H7) which lies on the crease of the wrist in a little depression between the bones of the hand and that of the forearm. Craving essence is a good remedy to support treatment.

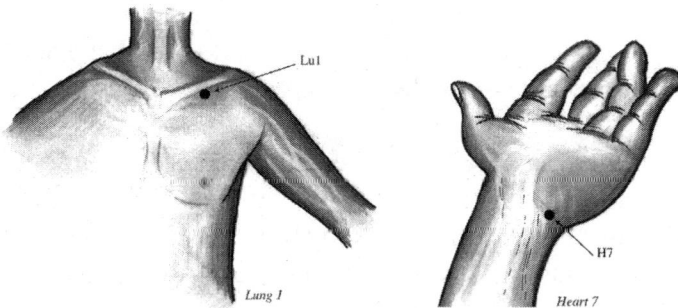

Image 10: Lu1 and H7

To locate H7, find the hollow depression that lies on the wrist (the side where your little finger is) between where your hand ends and your arm begins. (See image 10)

Worry affects the Lungs and Pancreas

Worry is unavoidable in the times that we live in when there is so much social instability! However, there are some pre-existing disharmonies in the body that could lead a person to be a constant worrier, even when there is nothing significant to worry about. This type of person worries excessively about everything. In TCM, we expect this to adversely affect the pancreas and the Lungs.

The first physical signs usually include stiff neck and shoulders, digestive problems, breathlessness and abdominal pain and distension. In the long-term it can also lead to asthma or other Lung disorders. Because worry drains and robs the body of energy, it can also lead to fatigue.

There's a good exercise to do before bed in cases of worry (especially if there is also insomnia): Cross the palms of your hands on your chest, take a few deep breaths feeling the movement of your chest caused by breathing, then during the next exhalation, sing the sound "aaaaah" quietly to yourself, drawing this out as long as is comfortable. You will feel the vibration under your palms. Imagine your lungs as bright white while you do this exercise. Also, taking each worry (especially those over which you have no control) and offering them to God in faith can be very useful. Say to yourself "I now offer this worry (name it) to you God and trust that you will resolve it in the way it must be".

It is also vital to cut sources of unrefined sugar that place further stress on the pancreas, and learn a technique such as yogic breath work.

One of my most striking cases involved a young mother who had been brought in by a relative. This woman had locked herself and her children in the house, and by the time family members had found her, she had not bathed, eaten or slept for days. The young children were taking care of themselves and trying to help their mother. At her first visit, she made no eye contact and didn't say a word throughout the entire session; only nodding her consent for treatment. Her hair had not been washed for a few weeks, she had not been to work, and she felt her world had fallen apart. By the end of the session she managed a smile. To my surprise, when I saw her the following week, she was neat and tidy and full of life, and she was back at work. She had a real sparkle in her eye! She then told me that she had been worried about her financial situation for quite some time, and then quite suddenly her depression and anxiety just began to spiral out of control (despite being on anti-depressants and anti-anxiety medication).

During the first session, I had picked up on adrenal depletion, and just one treatment had made a significant difference for her. She continued to see me for acupuncture after that, where we worked on correcting the damage that had occurred to the adrenals, lungs and spleen. At the time of writing this, she has been depression-free for a year and a half!

To strengthen the Lung and Spleen, massage the points Lung 7 (LU7) and Spleen 4 (SP4).

To locate Lu7 which is situated on the thumb side of your wrist, spread your thumb out away from the other fingers. In the little indent that is created at the wrist, place your index and middle finger to measure approximately two inches up on the arm.

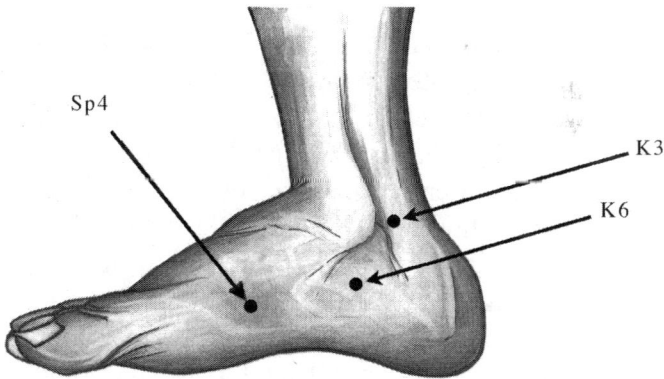

Spleen 4, Kidney 3 & Kidney 6

Image 11: Sp4, K3 and K6

Sp4 can be found on the inside aspect of the foot (big toe side) in a little hollow depression found halfway along.

Pensiveness affects the Pancreas and Heart

This is very similar to worry but involves constantly thinking about a situation, event or person. It's not so much worrying, but rather brooding and obsessive thoughts. It will cause similar symptoms as worry and the same exercises for worry apply.

Sadness or grief affects the Lungs and Heart

There are times and circumstances where we will not be able to avoid sadness and grief. Death or separation from a loved one leaves a gap and can have one feeling lost. Long term grief will lead to a weak voice, breathlessness, lung problems and weeping. It can adversely affect the immune system, leaving the person prone to infection. In women it can even cause the menstruation to cease.

Repressed sadness over a long period of time, when tears are unexpressed, will in the long run upset the fluid metabolism. In times of grief, it is essential to have a good support structure that we can move closer to in order to fill the gap. Depression and anxiety is a normal part of the grieving process, and although no time estimates can ever be put on grief, there is a point where support may be necessary.

An elderly lady came in to see me a while back about a much weakened immune system. She was getting one infection after the other, and was also developing very severe allergic responses where her tongue would swell up. She could hardly speak because her tongue was so swollen. It quickly became apparent that she was grieving for her husband who she had lost the year before. Interestingly, she had developed an infection which had damaged the lungs as well as the heart valves! She was quickly able to recognise the connection, although healing the allergies took a long time as she, understandably, found it very difficult to move through the grieving process.

Good points to massage for grief include Lung 1 (Lu1), Lung 7 (Lu7) and Heart 7 (H7), especially if there is chest tightness and difficulty breathing.

To locate Lu7 which is situated on the thumb side of your wrist, spread your thumb out away from the other fingers. In the little indent that is created at the wrist, place your index and middle finger to measure approximately two inches up on the arm.

Lu1 is located on the outside of your upper chest, at the level of the first intercostal space (that is, below the first rib) six inches from the midline of the body. (see image 10)

To find H7, find the hollow depression that lies on the wrist (the side where your little finger is) between where your hand ends and your arm begins. (See image 10)

Fear affects the Kidneys

The best example of this is uncontrolled wetting in acute fear, and it is also often seen in children who are anxious about a family situation (bedwetting). Chronic anxiety can manifest physically with palpitations, insomnia and night-sweating. Fear can also lead to chronic diarrhoea. In this case, acupuncture is very effective for those suffering from anxiety or panic attacks. In chronic fear there is usually a very white complexion. To strengthen the Kidneys, deep pressure on Kidney 3 (K3) can be helpful.

This point can be found one finger from the protruding bone on the ankle towards the heel in a soft depression. (see image 11)

Guilt affects the Kidneys and Heart

Guilt may arise when the person feels they have done something wrong or in those who always tend to blame themselves, even if they have done nothing wrong. Symptoms that may arise from long-term guilt include an uncomfortable and unsettling feeling in the chest, abdominal pain and distension. Guilt is often also expressed as depression, which may result in a nervous breakdown or in severe cases lead to suicide attempts. Just like Michael earlier on, guilt can wreak havoc not only the person who inflicts it on him/herself, but often on an entire family and friend network.

If there is guilt, the best remedy would be to talk to someone who you can trust or a trained counsellor, and this often also puts the situation into perspective. Points that may help resolve guilt include Du20 and H7.

To locate Du20, place your left thumb on the top of your left ear and your right thumb on the top of your right ear. Now place your fingertips on your head and feel for a hollow near the top center of your head.

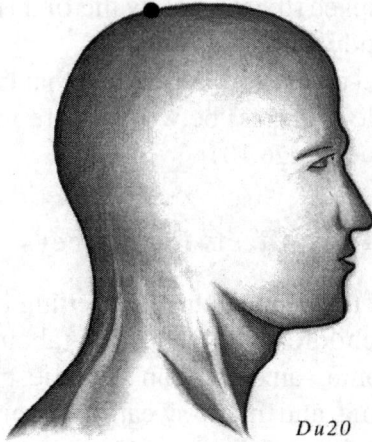

Image 12: Du20

To find H7, find the hollow depression that lies on the wrist (the side where your little finger is) between where your hand ends and your arm begins. (See image 10)

Modern stress affects the Kidneys

In TCM, when we refer to the Kidneys, it also includes adrenal function. It is said that when we push ourselves to physical or mental extremes, we deplete Kidney Qi. In the West, we can translate this to adrenal fatigue. In essence, it is like running low on car oil. The car will continue to run for a while after the oil has run out, but eventually the engine will burn out. In the body, we call this adrenal fatigue and it can happen after prolonged periods of stress or illness. In the same way as the car, some people continue to run at an extreme pace, despite their kidney/adrenal resources being exhausted. Once the adrenals are depleted, it can take a long time to repair.

Will power and drive is linked to the Kidneys in TCM. When patients complain to a TCM practitioner of feeling unmotivated or lacking the drive to follow through on dreams, there is often an underlying Kidney deficiency.

To nourish the Kidney, I suggest massaging Kidney 3 (K3) and Kidney 6 (K6).

K3 can be found one finger from the protruding bone on the ankle towards the heel in a soft depression. (see image 11)

K6 is found one finger below the protruding bone on the ankle in a tender depression. (see image 11)

Some diseases cause emotional disruption

Just as the energetic resonance of emotions can create disease, so the energetic resonance of disease can lead to emotional disturbance. There are many well documented causes of depression, for instance hypothyroidism, hormonal imbalance and even coeliac disease!

Anaemia, for instance, can make the person fearful and indecisive; this is more commonly seen in women. Hyperthyroidism can create extreme anxiety, irritability and agitation. Often, addressing a physical imbalance such as this can correct an emotional imbalance.

The Chinese clock in meditation

The Chinese organ clock explains when the best time is for 'maintenance' to be carried out on an organ. Just as a factory that runs 24 hours will shut down certain functions during a day for maintenance, our body does the same with the organs (see Chapter 7).

For healing a particular organ, meditation or massaging the acupressure points is best done at the time at which the 'maintenance' on that organ takes place. Take a few minutes each day to meditate on that organ with some deep breathing. The Gall Bladder and Liver are, however, during the night and one is not expected to wake up to do these exercises but care should be taken to be in bed by 10pm, and take a few drops of Milk Thistle just before bed. Also, avoid eating heavy greasy meals before bed.

Family cohesion

I had to write a few lines on family cohesion as this was another striking difference between my patients in the East and West. Generally, my patients in the East had very strong family units. It was often economically impossible for young couples to move out on their own, and they often remained with parents in the home, with the grandparents taking responsibility for raising the children. Although most people would balk at the idea of living with their parents-in-law, these young families often had more freedom because of having an extended family support structure. In addition, family members were offering emotional support to one another.

Before you put the book down, I am by no means suggesting that you move in with your mother-in-law, but research has shown that depression and anxiety are often linked to unsupportive family structures. There may be some benefit in rebuilding the family unit. This certainly was the case for me. I've always had a strained relationship with my mother, and it was only while living in the East (where family units are so very united) that it began to bother me. I decided to do something about it and now I am so very glad that I have. Healing family relationships can be extremely difficult when there is a lifetime of pain, anger and suffering. I think the important thing to remember is that you are doing the healing for yourself and not for the other person. In other words, you're healing family patterns for yourself. If there are patterns and issues that are ingrained, how do you change them and how do you begin talking, really talking, even if you have never done that before as a family?

I was once seeing both husband and wife separately as patients. The wife confided in me that her husband had been cold and distant throughout their relationship, and that she had a difficult time relating to him. They had been married for over 30 years now, and she resented the relationship that she had with this man. She had thought about leaving him, but her self-esteem was low and she worried that she would not cope without him (although in truth she had coped without his support for 30 years anyway).

Although she still loved him, she was past wanting to reconcile the relationship, and felt that the chasm between them was way too huge to ever cross over to him. Whenever I saw him, her husband was always very charming, kind and warm, and I wished that there was something to bring these two souls together, although I couldn't talk to him about it because of patient confidentiality. Then one day after I had known him for almost 6 months, he told me that he was having difficulties getting through to his wife. I felt huge relief because I was finally able to talk to him about this subject. He told me that he had no idea how to connect to his wife, and in recent months he had felt extreme resentment from her, which distanced him even more. Here were two people, both desperate to have a meaningful and deep connection, yet each believing that the divide was way too big.

Since the relationship was at rock bottom and there was nothing to lose, I suggested to the husband that he surprise his wife by creating a romantic evening together, and then to ask her whether she would be prepared to change the situation. If she said yes, they could then take steps together to build bridges. If she said no, he had at this stage very little to lose. He called me up a few days later to say that she had indeed said yes, and that they were going to go through a process of counselling. A few months later I received a thank you card signed by both of them.

Not all stories turn out this way, but we often have to take risks in relationships. There are often divides that begin to grow and chasms that get wider, but there are ways to change relationships around. I always think that life is so incredibly short. Why spend our very precious time in relationships that are unfulfilling or destructive? With some work on our own emotional terrain, either through counselling or personal introspection, our relationships become easier and more joyful and fulfilling!

What's holding you back?

There are unfortunately many reasons why in some cases people don't want to get better. The subconscious can at times, without our knowledge, invest in illness. There may be financial or emotional benefits to remaining ill, although the conscious mind does not always register this! I once had a woman coming in for acupuncture who had difficulties walking; she would improve for a little while, but then things would rapidly deteriorate. At one point she decided to discontinue treatment and we spoke about this. I was surprised since she had shown marked improvements on several occasions. She admitted to me that she had not worked for many years, and she was afraid that if her walking improved, she would be expected to return to the workplace, and that she had lost the confidence to do so. There was great ambivalence present. Although she was on some levels desperate to get better, the improvement would take her by surprise and raise anxieties that she couldn't deal with; she was so afraid of what getting better would really mean for her, that she would quickly deteriorate again. Once she recognised this, we could work with the anxiety about getting better and help ease her fears about getting back into the workplace.

I think it is essential to spend some time thinking about what your condition has made you do (give up work, exercise less), and of course also what it makes you do (stay indoors; lock yourself away), etc. Do this, however, without passing judgment on yourself. If, for instance, your condition has resulted in you giving up your job, don't berate yourself. Instead focus on what would need to change to be able to get you back to work (and maybe a different line of work is necessary). In other words, keep your thinking open and free of judgment.

Why do I feel stress physically in my body?

It is impossible to separate the mind, body and soul. When our mental health suffers, we will without doubt feel it physically within the body, and the other way around. Physical symptoms may be messages for you to change your life. They may be the first warning lights going on before a mental condition develops. Often physical symptoms are the way in which the mind tries to bring emotional issues to your attention. For example, you have been unhappy in your job for a very long time, but are unable to recognise or admit this. Then after a virus, you develop ME and find it impossible to go back to work. This may be your emotional body trying to tell you that this job/situation is not right for you.

Often in the past when I've not listened to my emotional radar, I've been hit over the head with a health issue that would not resolve until I sorted out my personal life. When I worked in the pharmaceutical industry many years ago, I knew at the back of my mind that I disagreed with the work ethics. At the time I started developing Irritable Bowel Syndrome (IBS) which completely stopped me working for several weeks at a time. As soon as I would go back into work, my IBS began to flare again. Leaving the industry did not seem like an option at the time. It felt as if I had wasted a degree and all my hard earned education. It took making the difficult decision to leave before my health began to improve and my IBS gradually resolved.

It can often be difficult to understand what the symptom is about. To get a clearer idea of what may be underlying your health condition, ask yourself the following questions. What does my condition stop me from doing? In my case the IBS stopped me from going to work. What does my condition make me do? For instance, does it make you more dependent on another person? Does it make you stay in the house? The answers to these questions may lead you to explore areas in your life where you need to change.

Loss, grief and bereavement

This book would not be complete without talking about grief, loss and bereavement. As I am writing today, I am catching glimpses of the Michael Jackson memorial service and I am reminded how deeply loss can move people. The news about his death broke about a week ago, and already there have been several fans committing suicide. This leaves me wondering how many of his fans, who have never even met the pop star in real life, could be moved to such drastic measures. I then have to remind myself how very powerful the experience of loss can be for each individual person.

When we think of loss we mostly associate it with death, but it is important to remember that other losses will often leave us with the same experience. I have a very dear patient who had surgery to remove a brain tumour. In the process, his face was disfigured. His partner reacted with a strong sense of grief. Although she still loved the man that he was, she understandably grieved for the change in his appearance.

Examples of losses are endless including death of a loved one (which includes animals), financial loss, loss of health, loss of a personality in the case of dementia, loss of worth, loss of dignity, loss of independence, loss of fertility etc.

The list is endless.

It is impossible to lose someone or something to which there has been an attachment without experiencing some pain. However, there are often pressures which prevent us from fully experiencing these painful feelings. People can cut off their feelings and deny the pain in many ways, including repressing emotion, moving home, drugs and alcohol abuse. However, in doing so it's like hanging a cloth over a piece of furniture so that we don't see it – but the piece of furniture is still there.

Grieving, although intensely painful, is necessary to help us move forward in life, so that we are able to look at that piece of furniture in a new light. Acknowledging the loss and working through grief requires courage, encouragement and support, so that you can express your pain and not carry it for the rest of your life. Once you are ready to do this, the possibility of healing will open.

With loss, we always have to adjust to a new environment. This may mean adjusting to a home without a partner, learning new skills to cope if the partner had performed certain roles such as driving or doing the household accounts. It may mean changing your lifestyle because of a financial loss or ill health. In loss there is often an overwhelming sense of loss of control; we have no control over the things that we lose. By making adjustments, we are able to regain some of the control and empower ourselves once again.

I see a lovely elderly lady who lost her husband to cancer some years ago. When we first met she was in severe depression. She was not only grieving the loss of her husband, she was also feeling that she was unable to cope. She was plagued by feelings of inadequacy. Her husband had played certain roles by taking care of their financial needs and decisions, driving, etc. She had never paid a bill in her entire life. Now she was unable to cope without him there and her health was suffering as a result. This is a very common situation after the death of a loved one. We worked on a way for her to start getting some of the control and power back. She got a friend in to help her understand how to manage her money, she also learned to drive (in her 70s!), and was slowly able to readjust to a new situation. Once again, this also takes enormous courage and the belief that you can learn to take control, even if you are in your 70s or 80s.

As humans, we are very resilient, resourceful and adaptable to changes in our environment. That is what has kept us going all these years and why humans are still around. You just have to remind yourself of that if you find yourself in a situation where adjusting seems like a mammoth task.

Finally, in doing this we learn not to forget about the person or thing that we may have lost, but ways in which to effectively continue living in the world. The idea is to give up the attachment to the deceased or lost person or thing, so that we can start to live life to the fullest again. In the case of death of a loved one, this is what the person most likely would like to see you do. Bereavement counselling can be very useful to help you move forward if you feel you are unable to do so yourself.

Self talk

It can be extremely difficult to think rationally when you are anxious. Here are some statements that may help with anxiety. Write them down, if they are relevant, and use them whenever you feel anxious. Repeat them often and frequently to yourself and in time they will become ingrained in your thinking pattern.

- "Right now I have uncomfortable feelings. They will pass and I will be all right. Anxiety is fleeting. It's just uncomfortable but not dangerous."

- "My anxiety, although frightening, does not have a hold of me. I am going to gently move my focus on what I need to do".

- "Although this seems hard now, it will become easier over time."

- "Even though my anxiety is powerful and frightening, it no longer holds the power over me that it once had."

CHAPTER 9

Lifestyle contributors

Meal times

Chinese physicians will tell you that what we do at meal times is very important. If one gets angry during meal times (when there are always mealtime rows), the anger will affect the Stomach causing stomach ulcers, indigestion etc. This could also be from stressful business lunches or just thinking too much about work when eating. If one gets angry after mealtimes (when one rushes back to a frustrating job after lunch), it can lead to intestinal problems such as IBS.

Meal times should be in a quiet and unrushed environment, although this can be a challenge for most people to achieve these days.

Alcohol

Alcohol use can be very tempting because of its numbing and relaxing action on the mind. However, long-term excessive alcohol consumption places a lot of stress on the liver, and can cause a liver imbalance which can further contribute to mental-emotional disturbances, leading to aggression or depression. If you find that you are using alcohol as an escape, it is necessary to find a practitioner who could help you work through emotions in a more constructive way. Because alcohol use is acceptable in our society, there is often denial when it comes to alcohol abuse. If you feel that you need to have a drink most days, you may need to explore if there is alcohol dependence.

There is also the question of alcohol intolerance. In some people who are alcohol sensitive, even a glass of wine can trigger anxiety or depression. However, this is rare and can be ruled out by having a food sensitivity test. There is also a common intolerance to sulphates in wines that could cause potential problems.

Chronic alcoholism may also have a serotonin link. Research has shown that alcohol initially increases serotonin nerve activity which makes the person feel good but long-term alcohol use actually impairs tryptophan absorption into the brain. Thus chronic alcoholism may involve a vicious spiral of an initial and brief alcohol induced increase of serotonin neural activity, with consequent feeling of well being, but with deteriorating baseline state of serotonin nerve activity.

Drugs

Any prolonged use of drugs that alter the mind, even the light drugs such as cannabis, can lead to mental confusion, lack of memory and concentration problems. They can also largely exacerbate a depression. Even a single dose of amphetamine (Speed or Crack) can result in permanent hyper-responsivity to stress. I worked with a young man who had been suffering severe depression, and it had taken us almost 3 months to get him depression-free when he met up with some old friends, and one thing led to the next, and he used a small amount of ecstasy. 2 days later I had a call from him and he was in a very severe state of paranoia. When he came in for a Resonance Biofeedback session, the reactivity measures on several neurotransmitters were all over the place, and it was almost impossible to get any balance back into the brain. It took him several months to recover from this incident, and he now had paranoia to deal with in addition to his depression. My view is that never, under any circumstances, take any drugs that can alter brain chemistry, even if it's just on a single occasion. The only thing to do is to completely avoid getting into any situations where there may be pressure to do so.

Sleep

Because serotonin (your feel good hormone) is converted into melatonin (sleep pattern regulator), it makes sense that depression can certainly affect sleeping patterns, and a change in sleep patterns is usually the first indicator before the mental symptoms of anxiety or depression register. For some, it means sleeping excessive amounts, for others it means early wakening (one of the signs of depression), or extreme insomnia. The disturbed sleeping pattern can then itself exacerbate anxiety or depression.

To regulate the sleep pattern, it is essential to stick to the same bed time each night, in order to re-establish the circadian rhythms. I find that the combination of acupuncture and the herb valerian is very effective in restoring sleep patterns. Tryptophan, which is the amino acid building block for both serotonin and melatonin, can also be supplemented. In chronic cases of sleep disturbance, testing melatonin levels can be very helpful.

10 Step Plan

1. Clear out junk from the diet including all processed and refined foods.

2. Look at what you're putting in. Make sure you're getting enough healthy nutrients in the diet. Add variety to the diet including fresh fruits and vegetables, seeds and nuts. Balance blood sugar.

3. Treat underlying physical conditions, especially allergies, metabolic issues and any bowel conditions. Go to www.acuhealthuk.com and fill in the mental health questionnaire to help identify possible contributing factors for your condition.

4. Find time for meditation and relaxation. Everyone enjoys different things – some like walking in a park, others painting or formal meditation. Do what suits you, and don't force yourself into formal meditation if the mind is not able to settle.

5. Engage in emotional healing – read books that support this or use therapies such as NLP (Neurolinguistic programming).

6. Make time for exercise, and even if you don't have the resources (time or money) to join a gym, take the stairs whenever you can, walk instead of taking the bus or driving.

7. Take responsibility for your own health!

8. Get enough sunshine; so make sure you get outside when the sun shines!

9. Get enough good sleep.

10. Get rid of energy drains.

In conclusion

There are many contributing factors that lead to anxiety, depression and panic. In my experience, there is always a solution. Life is too short to spend your resources (time and energy) in an anxious or depressed state. The world is a place where beauty, joy and laughter can always be found, and for this reason I believe it's so important to be fully engaged in life. Only when you are free of fear and sadness can you fully give yourself to life. We all deserve to have the life that we dream about, and so have a responsibility to ourselves and others to do what we can to create an abundant and rich experience of life. Your healing journey may not always be easy. You may have to deal with several complexities and challenges along the way, but always hold onto courage. It will see you through.

I hope that this book has helped to direct you onto a path of healing for yourself, and that the journey will bring you as much reward as I have seen it bring others.

Recommended Reading List

Forgiveness: The Greatest Healer of All, Gerald G. Jampolsky

Patrick Holford's New Optimum Nutrition for the Mind, Patrick Holford

Index

Acetylcholine, 13
Acupuncture, 88
Addictions, 55
Alcohol, 68, 141
Amygdalae:, 18
Antidepressants
  medications, 60
Anxicty, 3
Avena sativa, 93
Basal stress response, 105
Caffeine, 68
Chinese clock, 133
Coeliac, 34
copper, 43
Cortisol:, 51
Depression, 1
Dopamine, 10
Drugs, 142
Electrical circuits, 19
Emotional Freedom
  Technique, 96
Emotions, 124
Environment, 28
Essential Fats, 42
Exercise, 77
Family, 133
Female Hormones, 49
Food intolerance, 35
Fructose Malabsorption, 38
GABA, 7

Genes, 25
Grief, 137
Herbs, 93
Histadelia, 44
Homeopathy, 90
Homocysteine, 54
Hormonal changes, 47
IIypericum, 93
Lactose Intolerance, 36
Limbic system, 18
L-Tryptophan, 96
Magnesium, 72
Medications, 59
Melatonin, 9, 13
Migraine, 50
Neurotransmitters, 7
Noradrenaline, 11
Nutrient deficiencies, 72
Panic attacks, 3
Qi, 103
Qigong, 118
Reactive Depression, 56
Refined foods, 70
Resonance Biofeedback, 87
Seasonal Affective Disorder,
  46
Serotonin, 8, 9
Sleep, 80, 142
Stress, 28
Stress tolerance, 105

Sunlight, 79
Sympathetic Nervous
  System, 20
TCM
  Deficiency patterns, 116
  Excess patterns, 116
TCM diet, 108
Thyroid, 50, 51

Traditional Chinese
  Medicine, 101
Trauma, 28
Tryptophan, 40, 73
Vitamin B12, 73
Yin and Yang, 101
Zinc, 43